ALSO BY BRAD MATSEN

Jacques Cousteau: The Sea King

Titanic's *Last Secrets: The Further Adventures of Shadow Divers*
John Chatterton and Richie Kohler

Descent: The Heroic Discovery of the Abyss

Go Wild in New York City

Fishing Up North: Stories of Luck and Loss in Alaskan Waters

Planet Ocean: A Story of Life, the Sea,
and Dancing to the Fossil Record

Ray Troll's Shocking Fish Tales: Fish, Romance,
and Death in Pictures

Incredible Ocean Adventure (series for young readers)

DEATH AND OIL.

DEATH AND OIL

The True Story of the
Piper Alpha Disaster
on the North Sea

BRAD MATSEN

Pantheon Books, New York

All rights reserved. Published in the United States by Pantheon Books,
a division of Random House, Inc., New York, and in Canada
by Random House of Canada Limited, Toronto.

Pantheon Books and colophon are registered trademarks of
Random House, Inc.

Library of Congress Cataloging-in-Publication Data
Matsen, Bradford.
Death and oil : a true story of the Piper Alpha disaster on the North Sea /
Brad Matsen.
p.   cm.
Includes bibliographical references and index.
ISBN 978-0-307-37881-1
1. Offshore oil well drilling—Accidents—North Sea—History—20th
century. 2. Oil well drilling rigs—North Sea—History—20th century.
3. Oil wells—North Sea—Blowouts—History—20th century. 4.
Explosions—North Sea—History—20th century 5. Disasters—North
Sea—History—20th century. 6. North Sea—History—20th century. 7.
Aberdeen (Scotland)—History—20th century. 8. Disaster victims—North
Sea—Biography. 9. Suvival—North Sea—20th century. I. Title.
TN871.215.M36 2011   363.11'9622338190916336—dc22   2011011902

www.pantheonbooks.com

Jacket design by Brian Barth

Printed in the United States of America
First Edition
2   4   6   8   9   7   5   3   1

FOR BARBARA

Contents

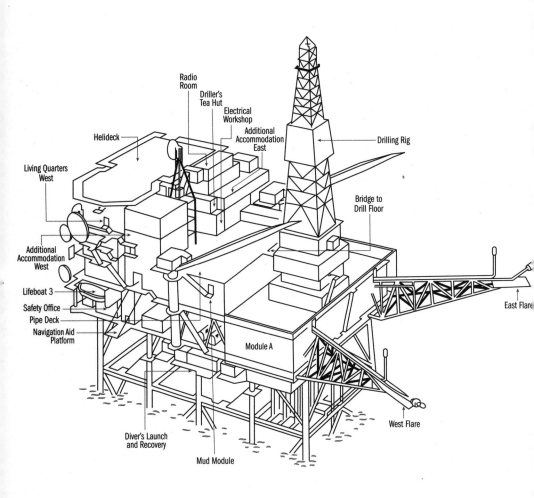

Radio
Room

Driller's
Tea Hut

Electrical
Workshop

Additional
Accommodation
East

Drilling Rig

Helideck

Living Quarters
West

Bridge to
Drill Floor

Additional
Accommodation
West

East Flare

Lifeboat 3

Safety Office

Pipe Deck

Navigation Aid
Platform

Module A

West Flare

Diver's Launch
and Recovery

Mud Module

Foreword

I began my research into the Piper Alpha tragedy in the autumn of 2008. For the first few weeks, I told friends who asked that I was writing the story of 162 men who died when an oil rig exploded on the North Sea. After many hours of reading the history of the Oil Age, I started saying that my book was also about the true cost of humanity's incredibly ill-advised addiction to petroleum. In just 150 years, our enchantment with oil has bloomed into a dependency on petrochemicals that frightens us all. I recited the famous quote by Sir Walter Scott about fishermen who died at sea—"It's not fish yer buyin', it's men's lives"—to make the point that responsibility for oil addiction and its consequences lies with each one of us. Not everyone agreed with my logic. Some people insisted that the oil companies and governments are more culpable than consumers because for a century and a half they promoted the use of petroleum for fuel, light, plastics, and fertilizer. They got rich doing it. The oil industry, they said, has also been notorious for trading off the safety of its workers and the health of the environment for profit.

By the time I finished a draft of *Death and Oil* in the autumn of 2010, the *Deepwater Horizon* had blown up, killing eleven men and releasing the biggest oil spill in history into the Gulf of Mexico. The rig was on charter to British Petroleum, drilling in five thousand feet of water to reach a pool of oil another twenty thousand feet down. When the news broke, most people outside the oil business were shocked by the extremes to which we now go to satisfy our demand for oil. We were further stunned when British Petroleum and Halliburton and the other contractors who helped BP drill the well blamed each other rather than accepting their own responsibility for the deaths of those men and the fouling of the Gulf.

The book that you are about to read is intensely personal. Men died on Piper Alpha. Their loved ones suffered unspeakable agony. A city was crippled by grief. The oil industry didn't miss a beat. The sadness and outrage I felt in the telling of this story was unavoidable, but my purpose is only to illuminate a powerful moment in the Oil Age from which we cannot simply look away. I have no doubt that Piper Alpha and *Deepwater Horizon* will happen again. Regardless of how we spread the blame, we can no longer ignore what is done on our behalf.

DEATH AND OIL

Autumn 1988

Six weeks after Bill Barron survived the world's deadliest oil rig disaster without a scratch he was up to a quart of whiskey a day. When he wasn't drinking or sleeping, he was digging a hole in the front yard of his cottage near the River Don north of Aberdeen. A few days after he started digging, people walking by could see only the top of his head bobbing up and down as he drove the shovel into the ground, brought his foot down on the top of it, and threw the dirt over his shoulder into what had been his garden. Sometimes, he just got in the hole and leaned on his shovel for a while. Neighborhood children stopped to watch. "What are you doing, Mr. Barron?" one of them asked. "I'm trying to get to Australia," Bill said, looking up out of his hole without a hint of guile in his weathered Highlander's smile. The adults on his street in Bridge O'Don who had known Bill for most of his life passed by quickly as though embarrassed by his apparently insane destruction of his property. All of them, of course, knew what had happened to him. In the Black Dog, the pub around the corner, they agreed that Bill was performing some kind of exorcism by digging his own grave over and over. The truth was that Bill just couldn't get through a day without a buzz or the physical work. This went on for months until his wife, Trish, gave him an ultimatum: Stop drinking and digging or I'm taking our daughter and leaving you.

One

CADDYSHACK

A few minutes before ten o'clock on the night of July 6, 1988, Bill Barron was in the cinema on Piper Alpha, Occidental Petroleum's champion oil rig 110 miles northeast of Aberdeen in the North Sea. He and a few other men were watching *Caddyshack,* a farce starring Bill Murray and Rodney Dangerfield. It was a golf movie. Golf was as central to the Scottish character as haggis, defiance, and whiskey, but everybody had already seen it at least once. Some of the men nodded off, tired after finishing their shifts. Barron was half asleep himself, huddled in the cinema out of boredom more than anything. A couple of the men were venting the tension of their workday by reciting punch lines along with the characters on the screen. When Rodney Dangerfield broke wind at a fancy dinner party, they tortured his words with an Aberdonian Doric brogue. "Whoa, did somebody step on a duck?"

The cinema was one of the concessions to comfort that publicity flaks for Occidental and the other oil companies liked to point out in interviews about life offshore. The room had theater seats just like the ones back in Aberdeen, with a video projection booth at the back of the room. The men were away from home for weeks at a time, subjected to the stresses of being surrounded by volatile, toxic chemistry, but they had hot showers, clean sheets, good food, and movies to make their days as bearable as possible. The message was that drilling the bottom of the ocean for oil was a technological challenge akin to taking a trip to the moon but that life aboard a rig was pretty good.

Bill Barron was drowsily watching Bill Murray whack the blos-

soms in a flower bed with a golf club when he picked up a faintly
unfamiliar sensation. Usually, the air on Piper Alpha carried the slick
fragrance of hydrocarbons and the constant noise of metal-to-metal
torment of a dozen kinds, but you got used to it. Sometimes, when
the wind shifted, or a big pump shut down, or a heavy load crashed
from a crane hook to the deck, the sensory blend changed just enough
to trigger an alarm in him. Barron remembered many moments during his ten years offshore when some distinct change in the smells
and sounds of the rig urged him to flee. What he heard in the
cinema was something new, a treble rumbling more visceral than
audible. He sensed it for a few seconds, woke fully, and sagged back
into the chair when it was gone.

Caddyshack had been showing on Piper Alpha for a week. Barron, who was not much of a golfer himself, absorbed the antics on
the screen with the same stoic good humor he brought to most of
the hours in his days. He was well-settled in himself as a working
man who was grateful to have had a good job for most of his life.
He did what he was getting paid for and led an essentially interior
existence, with a demeanor that was perfectly suited for living well
offshore. In the confined spaces of Piper Alpha, a man was better
off taking up as little room as possible. Barron never ceased to be
amazed that he could be eating a lamb chop for dinner, or enjoying
the tropical fish in their tanks in the galley, or watching a movie
with the world's biggest oil rig vibrating beneath him. He had gone
outside for a few minutes after dinner and knew that the air was
still and the sea calm. It was a beautiful evening in one of the most
unlikely places in which a man might find himself, especially since
the North Sea was usually a nightmare of rain, wind, and waves big
enough to shake the rig like it was made of twigs instead of steel.
Barron remembered storms so violent he was surprised to find himself still alive at dawn getting ready for another work day, nights
when sleep was impossible against the howling and shuddering of
gusts the men would all talk about in the morning. A hundred miles
an hour. A hundred and ten. Waves big enough to wash through
the upper decks carrying anything that wasn't bolted down into
the dark sea below. As the painting boss, Barron knew every inch

of Piper Alpha like no one else. Though he would always rather be at home in Aberdeen, he felt a sense of proprietorship about the rig that surprised him. It was, after all, just a giant machine absurdly plopped down in the middle of the ocean.

Piper Alpha was an awkward layer cake of steel on spindly legs that looked a lot like a gigantic moon lander from the *Apollo* missions. It had a bottom tier of four distinct aluminum modules—the wellhead; oil and gas separator pumps; gas compression pumps; and main power generators. Above these were the drilling derrick, a crane, and modules for storage, pressure tanks, and exhaust pipes. At the top of the rig were four tiers of crew accommodations that held a hundred and fifty sleeping cabins, a dining room, three game rooms, a library, the movie theater, and the administrative offices. The rig was seven hundred feet tall, four hundred and seventy-five feet of which were underwater, where the rig was anchored by steel and concrete to the seafloor.

The cinema was a twenty-five-by-twenty-five-foot corner of the accommodation module. The sleeping cabins would be familiar to third-class passengers on a ship, with berths for two or four men, a compact sink, shower, and toilet. Each deck had a locker room where the men shed their boots and coveralls after work in an effort to keep their sleeping cabins relatively free from the grime of the rig. The offshore installation manager, who was as omnipotent as a ship's captain, had his stateroom and an office on A Deck. It was the lowest in the accommodation stack, also housing fifteen cabins, a small gym with a treadmill, a rowing machine, a stationary bicycle, and an assortment of free weights. Off one corridor on B Deck were the offices for other supervisors, including Bill Barron; another changing room; the laundry; and twenty-one cabins. C Deck, where the cinema occupied one corner, held thirty-two cabins, two locker rooms, and two lounges with desks, reading chairs, and couches. D Deck was the top of the stack, with fourteen cabins, the sick bay, recreation room, rig-to-shore telephones, radio room, duty-free store, pantry, kitchen, and a dining room—known as the canteen—that could seat sixty men.

The thirty-by-thirty-foot room had serving hatches opening into the kitchen on the south wall and three square chest-high windows on the north. Against the facing wall were a pair of glass tanks in which an assortment of tropical fish added unlikely life and color to the institutional room. The kitchen could turn out six meals a day for as many as 250 men. A double door in the east wall of the galley led to a reception alcove. Corridors and staircases branched off to sleeping cabins, the sick bay, walk-in freezers, and the pantry. A duty-free bond shop that sold cigarettes, perfume, aftershave, and sweets was in a cubbyhole at the south end of the reception area. When the Dutch door to the shop was open, a model lifeboat with a coin slot in its deck sat on the service counter for donations to the Royal Lifeboat Society. The four decks of the accommodation module were linked by exterior steel stairways—called ladders in the nautical tradition—with handrails on both sides. In the winter, the ladders were icy and treacherous, but even in summer, oil and dampness coated every surface. A slip-and-fall on an oil rig could easily be fatal. After a few trips offshore, the instinct to reach for a handrail on any set of stairs never left a man.

The living conditions were as good as any in the British sector of the North Sea, though everybody envied the men on Norwegian rigs, which were much more luxurious. Offshore veterans relished the pranks they played on new men. A favorite was telling a rookie that a chopper was coming after dinner to take them over to a rig on the Norwegian side that had a disco and plenty of women for dancing. The helicopter landing officer was in on the joke. Most new guys spent a cold hour or two on the helipad waiting in the wind for the disco chopper before they figured it out.

Offshore workers took a job on Piper Alpha with trepidation. Even in calm seas, the rig trembled with an unsettling vibration. In heavy weather, it lurched and shuddered like it was about to come apart. It was noisy as hell and it stunk. All rigs smelled of sulfur, but Piper Alpha put out something extra that took the aroma into the realm of the vile. Everyone was leery, too, of Occidental's pride in the incredible production of its star offshore platform. The flow of oil to the pipeline terminal at Flotta on Orkney Island rarely fell below 100,000 barrels a day, worth from $1.5 to $4 million depending on the volatile global price for petroleum. On a great day, with every-thing working just right, Piper Alpha gushed 250,000 barrels of oil through its shore-bound pipeline. The record was 284,000 barrels, set just before demand slumped in the price wars of the early 1980s. The pressure to perform motivated some of the men who liked set-ting records, but it also increased tension on the platform and most of the workers could not care less how much money Occidental Petroleum made from their labor.

Offshore lore was as potent as storytelling in any other insular culture. Everybody knew that in June 1975 Piper Alpha killed its first man even before the rig was fully assembled. Parts of it were manufactured in Cherbourg, France, and loaded aboard a barge in the English Channel for shipment to the main fabrication yard at Ardersier, northeast of Inverness. In dense fog, a freighter sailed between the tug and barge and snared the half-mile-long towing cable. The freighter broke apart, the pieces went down in minutes, and one of its six crewmen was never found. Maritime disasters have happened regularly on the English Channel and the North Sea forever, but what made this one big news was Occidental Petro-leum's earlier stream of press releases crowing about their gigantic rig. It would be the heaviest ever built, erected in deeper water than any oil platform in history. During two years of construction, work-ers called the massive assembly of girders, rails, and pilings "The Monster," but for most of them there was also a sense of pride. They were after all building the biggest thing of its kind in the world.

In 1982, three more men died when a gangway collapsed between Piper Alpha and the support platform, *Tharos*, that was alongside as a floating hotel for extra workers. Then, in March 1984, an explosion ripped through the production modules, forcing an emer-gency shutdown and the evacuation of the 175 men aboard at the time. A few men were hurt, four seriously, but if the explosion had not happened at lunchtime when most were upstairs in the canteen, many would have died. Consistent with the culture of secrecy that governs life offshore, Occidental never revealed the conclusions of an inquiry into the accident. Accidents like the explosion on Piper Alpha killed and maimed men with terrible regularity on the North

Sea; Occidental, British Petroleum, Shell, Texaco, Chevron, and the other companies managed publicity with the same ruthless efficiency they brought to extracting oil and gas.

The rigs themselves were audacious. Piper Alpha's jacket—the framework attached to the seafloor that supported the production, drilling, and accommodation modules—weighed 28 million pounds. It stood 552 feet tall when upright but had been built while lying on its side to reduce effects of gravity as it grew. The construction of such a massive assemblage of steel would have been perfect for the shipyards of Glasgow, Belfast, and the River Clyde, which, in the early 1970s, were crumbling ruins as heavy steel construction migrated to Asia. The American oil barons who were orchestrating the extraction of the North Sea bonanza wanted nothing to do with still-powerful unions in the British shipyards. Instead, they ordered their rigs from companies which agreed to build fourteen new fabrication yards around the United Kingdom. Each was an employment juggernaut that almost overnight salvaged Great Britain's labor force from the depths of a recession that had idled a third of the nation's workers. Most of the men learned to be pipe fitters, welders, boilermakers, concrete workers, painters, X-ray inspectors, or took up one of the dozens of other trades on the job. Fewer than one in a hundred of the twenty-five thousand men and women in the fabrication yards were in unions.

Life in the yards was akin to what their ancestors had endured in wartime factories driven by urgency: overtime, meat and potatoes, and cramped living quarters in remote outposts. One of the biggest challenges was simply finding places for fourteen thousand men to sleep on the outskirts of a village of a hundred and fifty people. Off the coast near several fabrication yards, the oil companies moored chartered cruise ships to handle the flood of men. In others, the workers' first job was to build their own barracks while living in tents or camp trailers. For many of the men, a job in one of the fabrication yards was a ticket to what most of them assumed would be more well-paid work offshore when they finished building the rigs.

Piper Alpha's jacket left the Ardersier fabrication yard on specially built barges in early June 1975. The rust-colored monster looked like the steel framework of a tall building lying on its side as it moved slowly past the ecstatically green slopes of the Highlands, out of Moray Firth, and into the North Sea. The weather forecast was good. At just over one knot an hour, the four tugs towing the jacket took almost a week to reach the site that had been carefully selected by Occidental's geologists as the heart of the field. On the last day, the weathermen turned out to be wrong. Dawn broke with a howling ninety-knot gale and sixty-foot waves. They arrived at the latitude and longitude specified months ago by the geologists, but couldn't hold their position. In desperation, they dumped the jacket as close as they could to the site of the template that divers had installed on the seafloor to which the jacket would be anchored.

The next day, wind and sea returned to normal for June and the job of permanently fixing Piper Alpha to the seabed began. On the surface, pile drivers drove steel shafts through sheaths at the bottom of each of the rig's four giant legs, through the template, and 390 feet into the earth. Fortunately, the battering the jacket took the day before when it hit the bottom in the wrong place didn't bend the legs out of position. Divers, saturated with nitrogen and living in pressurized habitats for month-long shifts, completed the anchoring job by welding the legs in place. They illuminated the seafloor around the rig with enormous lights, transforming the darkness into a technoscape reminiscent of the monolith scene on the moon in the movie *2001: A Space Odyssey*. Working alone and in pairs, the divers joined steel with beads of tungsten welding rods ignited by cables from the surface. When the rig was as firmly emplaced as any man-made structure on earth, they fitted the thirty-six sleeves through which the drills and the pipe from each wellhead would be guided.

Hundreds of men worked on the hookup crew, swarming over and under the rig as the production and accommodation modules, drilling floor, derrick, and ten thousand tons of heavy equipment were mounted on the jacket. Occidental parked *Tharos* alongside as the headquarters for the hookup and a hotel for the men who were not billeted aboard one of the many other support ships and barges that came and went. On *Tharos*, and among the specialized

crews who came out from Aberdeen to link Piper Alpha to the oil
it had come to extract, the word spread about the plague of already
urgent repairs needed on the giant new rig. Corrosion had been
eating at the steel since it was laid in place in Ardersier. Welds were
separating or pitted. The immense pressures of moving the jacket
and plunging it into the sea had broken some of the cross members and warped others. Grumbling on an industrial job site was as
natural to the work gangs as breathing, but by the time Piper Alpha
was ready to drill its first well in November 1976, the grumbling
had turned to genuine concern that the rig was fatally flawed. "We
could see that Oxy had taken a lot of shortcuts on that rig, the way
they added cross braces after the jacket was finished, cracks in the
steel as soon as it was in the water, lots of corrosion," said one of
the men on the hookup crew. "It was a wreck of a job. The joke was
that the Piper would be the first fucking oil rig on the fucking moon
when it blows."

Even on a rig with a bad reputation, life offshore suited Bill Barron.
He didn't believe that Piper Alpha was any more dangerous than
any other rig on the North Sea. Thousands of men had been injured
or killed on the rigs, many of them because they weren't paying
attention or were taking unnecessary risks. Barron knew how to
handle himself pretty well in places where most people would be
uncomfortable. He was a slow, careful walker, a man whose eyes
never stopped moving when he wasn't absolutely sure he was safe.
Barron believed he had survived to be a fifty-two-year-old painting
boss on an oil rig by paying attention. Though he was a small man
at five and a half feet, he was quick and muscled, with a boxer's
reaction time. Barron came from country people tied to the Scottish
Highlands by generations of farmers, warriors, and seamen. Most
of the men in his family trickled into construction work that took
them from the farm to a succession of bridges and dams during the
prosperity of postwar reconstruction that crested in the late 1950s.
Barron had seen a wearying future for himself in rural Scotland so
he joined the army as soon as he was old enough to legally sign his
own name, thinking he would make a career of it. In the elite Royal

Highland Regiment—the Black Watch—Barron soldiered for three years in Kenya and Germany. In 1960, he earned a coveted assignment at Holyroodhouse in Edinburgh, but guarding the queen and her palace bored the hell out of him and the shine went off his plan to stay in the army. When his enlistment ended, Barron found a job on a concrete crew that was part of the first attempt by England and France to link the two countries with a tunnel under the English Channel. When the first Chunnel attempt failed, he stuck with the Sika concrete company which took him to jobs building tunnels in coal mines in Wales and dams in Scotland, as well as a string of bridges all over the British Isles. He met and married Patricia, Trish. They had Melanie in 1970. Home life was a succession of his months-long absences while Trish worked in a laundry in Aberdeen, tended their cottage in Bridge O'Don, raised their daughter, and welcomed him home for an occasional two weeks with the plodding resignation of a ship captain's wife. Barron was doing well enough to own a house, well enough to relax and putter when he was home, but as he drifted into his forties he wanted more time in Aberdeen and less time in construction camps. Like everyone else, he watched warily as the Americans with their hats and indecipherable accents began to arrive on the Northeast coast of Scotland in the late sixties. The oil thing looked like a boomer, most people thought, but the word up and down Union Street in Aberdeen was that it would be a flash in the pan, here today, gone tomorrow. Barron kept his job with Sika until 1977 when two weeks at home for every two weeks spent on a job offshore was irresistible. By then, too, it looked like the oil business was going to be around longer than anybody figured.

Life at home got better for the Barrons when Bill went to work offshore. Trish was sleeping beside her husband much more often than any time during the past twenty years. Melanie was heading into adolescence with her father in her life. Bill's love of hunting and shooting with his pair of spaniels had existed mostly in longing memory, but every two weeks they were more real to him than ever before. He had always liked tinkering with cars, too, and bought himself a classic black and orange Vauxhall Victor, one of the last of its kind. Life on the rigs was toxic for countless marriages in Aberdeen but Bill and Trish were somehow immune from the plague. When Barron asked himself why, he always came up with the same answer: I just love my wife.

Offshore, Barron was known as a good boss. He and his painting crews called their endless work "chasing the rust," which was the truth about what they did. Without constant sand blasting, wire brushing, corrosion coating, and painting, a steel oil rig exposed to saltwater and the weather would be a derelict in a few years. His crews could only work when their highly flammable coatings and paints were nowhere near any open flame or electrical arc. Some days he needed two men, some days he needed a dozen. On the night that Barron sat watching *Caddyshack* in the cinema he had just sent eight of his men ashore. The installation of a new pipeline and maintenance on a gas pump was going to close off most of the rig for the coming week. Three painters were still aboard but Barron wasn't sure what they were going to do the next day.

Of the 226 men on Piper Alpha, 160 were off-duty that night. For twelve hours, until they went back to work at six in the morning, they would go about the routines of eating, sleeping, and passing the time. They had careful boundaries with each other, knowing that in close quarters life could be grim when conflicts or misunderstandings occurred. Fifteen years into the North Sea oil boom, most of the bad apples had been fired or quit and the oil companies and contractors kept careful track of which men were trouble offshore. The worst thing that could happen to a man on a rig was to be branded NRB—Not Required Back—which put him on that particular company's Black List. If he found another job and fouled up again, he was likely to find himself on what everybody called the White List, which meant no company on the North Sea would let him in the door. Organized labor tried to fight back, but less than one percent of all men offshore were in a union so the Black Lists and White Lists endured. It was nothing like the early years of the boom when any man with a pulse could work offshore. In those days, the danger of living on a platform in the middle of the ocean was compounded by personality conflicts, grudges, and an atmosphere more like a prison block than a temporary home. Now, in the much more sedate days and nights of the production era, off-duty men did laundry, read in their cabins, played snooker or cards, went to the movies, or slept. Every one of them had been searched for drugs, alcohol, weapons, and other contraband known to disrupt the fragile society on an oil rig. Betting on cards, pool, or other games was forbidden.

In the lounge on D Deck, Eddie Crowden was in one of the six phone booths talking to his girlfriend, Kay Harney. Phone calls were free and among the most precious of perks offshore. Crowden was forty-seven and recently divorced with four daughters, the youngest of whom was eighteen. On Piper Alpha that night, he counted the hours until he would see Kay. Harney, also forty-seven, was divorced with two children. Crowden was an electrician whose primary job was keeping tabs on the batteries in the lifeboats and other safety equipment. It was repetitive, endless work, he complained to Kay, a job that bored the hell out of him, but he couldn't walk away from the money. Unlike most of the men who worked for one of the two dozen contractors on Piper Alpha, Crowden was on the Occidental payroll. In the subtle caste system on a rig, company men were a cut above contractors. Crowden had one of the better staterooms, with a window, had only one roommate, and knew from week to week where he would be working. Still, he spent every day aboard the rig wishing he were back in Portlethen, the fishing village south of Aberdeen where he and Kay lived. Crowden was a big, beefy man, suited to the fishing life of his ancestors who faced danger but depended on the freedom of a boat on the open sea to make their lives worth living. Before the boom, a thousand or so people lived on the little harbor with its fleet of day boats at a pace that was not much different than it had been for hundreds of years. After the oil, the population swelled to more than five thousand scattered around the village and in the nearby uplands. The women of Portlethen and the other seabound villages of Northeast Scotland were used to welcoming their men home and sending them away again, but there was something different in the way the oilmen came and went. It might have been the money, or the arrival of so many people from away, but in a place where divorce had only recently been unthinkable, lying and deception suddenly seemed to warp many marriages. Everyone heard the stories of men who added two or three days to their time offshore so instead of coming straight home they could fetch up in Aberdeen, an old Calvinist city that had become a Klondike of bars, casinos, strip clubs, and hotels that asked no questions.

After Eddie Crowden told Kay Harney how bored he was with his job on Piper Alpha, she told him that her darts party with the girls seemed a waste without him giving her the eye from the bar. Then they talked about getting married when things settled down. It had been coming up a lot lately, and it was Kay who seemed to be dragging her heels. Neither of them was really sure what when-things-settled-down meant beyond the comfort of the words that warbled over the satellite telephone. Just before 10 p.m., Eddie and Kay ended their day with promises.

Two

PUMPING MONEY

On Piper Alpha's production deck, fifty feet below Eddie Crowden and Bill Barron, the endless work of extracting crude oil went on through the night. Sole responsibility for keeping it flowing in from the wells and out through the pipelines during the night shift rested on Bob Vernon. Vernon was descended from working men who for generations had hammered, poured, smelted, and refined whatever humanity demanded. When that demand vanished after the Second World War, tens of thousands of men from Falkirk, Vernon's hometown, and the rest of the industrial centers of Great Britain were cast into the difficult business of reinventing themselves. Like so many, Vernon had been saved by North Sea oil. He learned how to run big machines, manage crews of men, and cope with the pressure of life offshore, eventually landing one of the top jobs on the world's biggest oil rig. Unlike the drillers, painters, welders, divers, maintenance men, plumbers, cooks, and stewards who were beholden to contractors selling services to Occidental, Vernon and the others who manned the control room on Piper Alpha worked directly for the company.

Vernon had taken over as Piper Alpha's lead production operator for the twelve-hour shift that began at six in the evening. He and his relief, known as his back-to-back, Harold Flook, never encountered each other beyond the confines of the rig and the chopper lounge at Aberdeen airport, but they both brought the practiced competency of lifers to their jobs. They always met a half hour or so before each shift started to go over the logs, work orders, notes, and maintenance records. Their conversation was mundane, but both men paid close attention to the details of their handoff. An oversight about the inner workings of the rig could be dangerous or at the very least slow the flow of crude oil to shore.

Piper Alpha was the most productive oil rig on the North Sea. Vernon initialed a production log attesting that it had pumped 138,294 barrels of crude oil to the Occidental terminal on Orkney Island during the previous twenty-four hours. Neither man bothered to compute the value of the oil, but at that day's price of $14 a barrel it was worth $1,936,116. That was only half of what Occidental expected Piper Alpha to produce in twenty-four hours, but Vernon wasn't worried about the shortfall. Like all offshore rigs, Piper Alpha was in a constant state of repair, alteration, and improvement. In the middle of the summer, when the foulest weather on the North Sea let up, the pace of the work maintenance intensified at the expense of production tallies.

Piper Alpha was not only a drilling and production platform but a junction station for gas flowing from two other platforms. Texaco's Tartan, twelve miles to the east, and Occidental's own Claymore twenty-two miles to the southwest, pumped their gas through Piper Alpha to shore. That summer, Occidental was hurrying to connect a third rig in the giant Frigg gas field, Chanter, to Piper Alpha's pipelines. When the work on the Chanter pipeline was done, all four rigs would be sending gas to shore through a platform known as MCP-01, a giant pump on a concrete tower attached to the seafloor. Denied even a name, MCP-01's main function was to boost the pressure in the pipeline from Piper Alpha and the other rigs to keep the gas moving through two thirty-two-inch pipes on its long journey to shore. Every gas-fired furnace, fireplace, and factory in the British Isles depended on the steady flow of North Sea gas.

Installing the Chanter pipeline and performing summer maintenance at the same time was tricky business. Deepwater divers tended by two extra ships, *Maersk Cutter* and *Lowland Cavalier,* were laying pipe on the seafloor. From the support platform *Tharos,* other divers were guiding the line up to Piper Alpha's pumps. A team of inspectors had been on Piper Alpha for a month to pressure test each of the three-hundred-some valves on the rig. Bill Barron's painters and crews of maintenance men were fighting their constant battle against rust and corrosion. Divers stationed on Piper Alpha were doing pretty much the same thing to the four hundred feet of the gigantic steel structure that was underwater. Drillers were sinking no new wells from Piper Alpha, but they constantly deepened, reamed, and cleaned the holes already bored into the crude oil below. Strictly speaking, rigs only drilled for oil. Piper Alpha was technically a production platform, but in the offshore vernacular, any fixed, floating, drilling, or production platform on the ocean was usually just a rig.

Piper Alpha was created to drill up to thirty-six wells and pump oil and gas from a subterranean reservoir on which Armand Hammer, the majority owner of Occidental Petroleum, had bet his company. Occidental and a consortium of minority partners including another oil buccaneer, J. Paul Getty, had successfully campaigned for a license to drill in two prime tracts of the North Sea. They paid the nearly bankrupt government of Great Britain an undisclosed amount of cash up front and promised a royalty share of the field's production if they struck oil. Occidental would also owe the British treasury 40 percent of its profits in taxes. In oil company boardrooms, the hot gossip was that Hammer and his cronies had worked out a sweetheart deal through the foreign office because of Hammer's stature as an international financial legend with near-ambassadorial privileges from the American government.

Hammer, Getty, and their geologists had a pretty good idea that the tracts they had leased held oil, but they didn't know exactly how much. The summer of 1972 had been a long one for the oil tycoons. Their exploratory drilling rig *Ocean Victory*, chartered at $40,000 a day, bored two dry holes in three months before hitting a layer of porous Jurassic rock eight thousand feet down. In the heart of the earth's crust, they had found a billion-barrel pool of low-sulfur crude, the kind of discovery called an Elephant in the parlance of the high-stakes oil game. Low-sulfur crude was the best kind because what came out of the ground as a thick slurry could be easily refined into marketable oil and gas. During the middle of the dinosaurs' 160-million-year run, the volatile blend of oil and gas seeped into what geologists called Piper sandstone. Now, with the biggest oil rig ever built—the alpha rig of the Piper field—he had come to take as much of that oil and gas out of the ground as quickly as he could. "Wait until you see what the North Sea discovery does for this company," he told his public relations man. "I'm a genius."

Armand Hammer liked making money but, even more, he savored the challenges of coaxing oil and gas from one of the world's most notorious patches of ocean. The North Sea is a shallow spur of the Atlantic covering the northern European continental shelf to average depths of 321 feet, and a maximum depth, in a trench off the Norwegian coast, of 2,300 feet. It is a vestige of tectonic spreading, a geologic stretchmark sculpted by more recent glaciation that created humps and holes so familiar to navigators that they had earned names: the Long Forties, Ling Bank, Devil's Hole, Vikingbank, the giant Dogger Bank, and, near where Armand Hammer found oil, Witch Ground. Until the oilmen arrived, those irregularities in the seafloor created the old world's most productive fishing grounds, feeding the people of the British Isles, Scandinavian Peninsula, and continental Europe for a thousand years. They also produced wicked sea conditions as wind-driven currents roared counterclockwise around the shallow basin to create slow-moving but enormous waves most of the year. For mariners, the North Sea has always been synonymous with terrifying weather. Even landlubbers feared it. On the night of January 31, 1953, hundred-mile-an-hour winds and eighty-foot seas overwhelmed seawalls, dikes, and levees and killed more than twenty-five hundred people in the coastal villages of southern England and Holland. The storm drove hundreds of thousands from their homes, many of whom never returned. The North Sea had simply beaten them.

The primordial sludge Piper Alpha sucked from the earth was almost useless until it was separated into compounds that could be ignited, exploded, or transformed into countless other substances upon which modern life depends. Hydrocarbons—oil, gas, tar—form when microscopic animals and plants decompose after being trapped many millions of years in accumulating mud. When heated and distilled, it separates according to the number of carbon atoms that form the finished products. Wax, coke, tar, and asphalt with seventy or more carbon atoms in each molecule liquefy at 1,112 degrees Fahrenheit and are drawn off first as the superheated crude flows out of a distillation boiler. Heavy bunker fuel oil separates at 700 degrees, followed by lubricating oil, diesel, kerosene for jet fuel, lamp oil, gasoline, methane, ethane, propane, and butane at lower temperatures of down to 104 degrees. Chemical engineers have figured out how to manipulate the carbon molecules in crude oil to yield plastics, fibers, electrodes, and hundreds of other modern essentials that bear no resemblance at all to what comes out of the ground.

The crude oil that flows from wells around the world has as many variations as wine vintages, depending on the levels of sulfur and other impurities that affect its conversion into petroleum products. Like the delicious litany of grapes and vineyards that delight oenophiles, unrefined oil is known by names specific to its source and its degree of sweetness—the relative absence of sulfur and other compounds that impede the distillation process. The sweeter the crude, the more valuable it is because less energy is required to transform it. On world oil futures exchanges, traders buy and sell more than 150 different kinds of crude, including Argentina Sauces, Chile Magallanes, Chinese Shengli and Taching, Colombian Limon, Venezuelan Lago Treco, Mexican Isthmus, Arab Heavy, Arab Light, West Texas Sour, East Texas, Louisiana Blend, and Alaska Sweet. In 1971, Shell had discovered the first oil in the northern North Sea and named its first rig after the Brent goose, a dark-feathered bird that breeds in the Arctic, hence the name of the vintage of oil pumped from that part of the ocean. The crude from Occidental's Piper field, which carried relatively low amounts of sulfur, was known as Brent Sweet Crude or London Brent.

The four production modules on Piper Alpha had been assembled onshore, brought to the standing steel jacket on barges, and mounted like the components of a huge computer sliding into precision-built slots. The 40-by-20-by-150-foot rectangular modules were welded to the jacket with their floors at the eighty-three-foot level above the surface of the sea. Production Module A was the easiest to identify

because it was the only fully enclosed module of the four, separated from the rest of the rig by heavy blast walls. In it were the
wellheads that linked Piper Alpha to the explosive hydrocarbons
rising up through miles of pipe from the subterranean depths. Even
with blowout protectors called Christmas trees on each wellhead,
A Module was the most ominous place on the rig. As though to
illustrate the hellish potential of the stuff Piper Alpha brought to
the surface, a pair of two-hundred-foot-long steel booms projected
from A Module's east and west corners. At the end of each, a gas
flare burned day and night to dispose of gas that was not shipped to
shore or burned on the rig for its own power.

When Occidental laid its plans for installing the Chanter pipeline
and the summer maintenance of Piper Alpha, Armand Hammer listened to arguments for shutting down the whole rig for a month to
get the jobs done. In the end, Hammer decided on a compromise.
Piper Alpha would keep the oil flowing but pump no gas to shore.
The rig would harvest some of the gas from its own wells to power
itself and burn off more than thirty times the normal amount. When
Bob Vernon and his night shift came to work, the flares sounded
like a thousand jet engines and looked like roiling tongues of fire
intent on biblical punishment. All over the rig, the men could taste
the heat of them.

From the top of A Module, the drilling derrick rose to 225 feet
above the sea, the highest point on Piper Alpha. The familiar quad-
rilateral pyramid had been the dominant icon of the oil age since
its beginnings in Titusville, Pennsylvania, in 1859 when Edwin
Drake drilled his first well in a muddy field. Like so many other ele-
ments of an offshore platform, the derrick's function was simple but
expressed on a gigantic scale. To feed the drill from the rig to the
oil eight thousand feet down, thirty-foot sections of thick-walled
pipe had to be raised vertically from the deck, screwed into the section below it, and lowered into the well. When pulling the pipe up
to change a drill bit or reline the walls of a well, the process was
reversed. At the top of the derrick, tended by a man stationed on
a platform to guide the drilling pipe, a clawlike crane latched onto
each section of pipe and pulled it up.

B Module was a much closer approximation of the metaphoric

heart of the machine. Here were the rig's critical veins, arteries, and organs. A thirty-foot-long, heavy steel intake manifold channeled the crude oil from the wellheads to a pair of enormous pressurized cylinders in which pumps and gravity separated the water, oil, and gas. The water went back into the sea. The oil was pumped into the thirty-inch main pipeline for its 130-mile trip to shore. The gas went over to C Module next door for purification, compression, and injection into a sixteen-inch pipeline connected first to the Claymore rig and on into the main gas pipeline to St. Fergus in Scotland. C Module was the busiest looking of the four, with a confusing array of coolers, pumps, two kinds of compressors, storage tanks, and control boards occupying floor space equivalent to half a football field.

In D Module at the north end of the production deck, two turbines the size of railway locomotives generated the power Piper Alpha consumed to extract the crude oil and gas, separate it, and pump it to shore. The massive generators, which could run on either gas or diesel fuel, also produced the electricity for the lights, outlets, and communications for the rig. The turbine exhaust was as big around as the engine of a 747, projecting from the side of the rig with aluminum ducting to direct the blast downward into the sea. Next to the exhaust, two of Piper Alpha's six lifeboats hung from davits. Another two lifeboats were tucked into niches at the ends of the production deck, two more mounted on the deck above under the accommodation modules. Each of the lifeboats could hold forty-seven men. Thirteen twenty-five-man life rafts, 519 life jackets, and twelve knotted climbing ropes completed the inventory of escape equipment salted around the rig.

During the shift handoff, Bob Vernon scanned the wall-mounted schematics of Piper Alpha's four production modules. What to ordinary people were baffling mazes of steel were, to him, elegant concoctions of pumps, valves, combustion chambers, and pipes for turning crude into what oilmen called product. He noticed from the production log that the valve inspectors were almost done. They were down to their last pressure safety valve, marked on the schematic of the rig's plumbing as PSV 504. The valve's job was to contain gas flowing at a specific pressure and close tightly if the pressure rose or fell beyond its design limits. PSV 504 was one of two valves protecting two pumps that were the final stage before shipment of gas and oil from the rig. At least one of those two pumps had to be running twenty-four hours a day or Piper Alpha would have to shut down. Everyone who worked for Occidental knew that on a visit to Piper Alpha, Armand Hammer had famously quipped, "All that money being pumped ashore stops if you shut down this rig. We don't let that happen."

While Vernon came on duty, the men stationed in the rig's main control room were also changing the guard. The control room was a gray cubicle on a mezzanine above D Module at the 107-foot level. On one wall were panels of breaker switches, alarm lights, and buttons arrayed on a diagram of the rig's primary production and power systems. On the other wall, across an aisle barely big enough for a man to sit in an office chair, was a desk and an electrical panel of alarms and circuit breakers for systems in the accommodation modules. Geoff Bollands, one of Vernon's production engineers, ticked through the status of the turbines, power plants, valves, compressors, condensers, and pumps. Bollands was English, in his early forties, and one of a dozen men from the valley of the Tees River in North Yorkshire who worked on Piper Alpha. He was a churchgoing family man whose wife and three children had waved him away a week earlier when he drove north to Aberdeen with three other Teeside men headed for the rig. Bollands was on the Occidental payroll, second-in-command to Vernon, and an expert on the power turbines and main pumps. He had an instinctive feel for the sounds and vibrations of the rig. As he looked over the lights and switches on the control board, Bollands could sense the general health of the growling machine that surrounded him. Everything was fine. There was nothing better than signing into his shift with a well-behaved oil rig. The only thing unusual was that gas production to shore was still shut down. He made a mental note to check in with Bobby Richard, the gas production chief, to find out what was going on in C Module.

As Bollands meandered through his routine hand off, Bobby Richard clomped into the control room. It was going to be a slow night because most of the machinery for compressing and pumping gas was idle. The man he was relieving hadn't noted in his log whether gas condensate pump A was still off-line or not, but the work was supposed to have been finished on the day shift. Richard was not concerned. He initialed the log, officially taking over his desk. Satisfied that everything in the control room was as it should be, Richard left for a walk-around to visually inspect his machinery.

Five hours after Vernon, Bollands, and Richard came to work, another of their countless twelve-hour shifts was unfolding predictably. Nothing out of the ordinary marred the routine of sitting in front of the control panels, taking turns on tea breaks, and popping out onto the catwalk alongside the lifeboats for air. By 9:30 p.m., the sun had dropped below the horizon but the sky still glowed with the last of the day's light. The steel-gray sea below was strangely calm, even for a midsummer evening.

Bollands and Vernon were in their swivel chairs at the main board when a red bulb on the central panel flashed. Both men were as familiar with the lines and lights on the board as they were with the palms of their own hands and this one could mean real trouble. It was coming from the sixty-eight-foot level where the plumbing for injecting the oil and gas into shore-bound pipelines converged. The breaker on one of two critical pumps down there had tripped. Before they could react, a klaxon punctuated the flashing red light, raising the level of the alarm from routine to urgent. Vernon was out the door in seconds, leaving Bollands poking at the button under the flashing light to silence the klaxon. That done, Bollands snatched a handheld VHF radio from its charger on the desk and called Bobby Richard. If something was queer with the gas compression equipment, Richard would be the best man to figure it out.

From the control room in the mezzanine above D Module, Vernon dashed across a catwalk and down a ladder into C Module, his arms outstretched to grab both railings as he descended at a trot. Before he reached the bottom of the ladder, he heard the rattle of another set of fast-moving footsteps behind him, glanced over his shoulder, and saw Richard come around the corner from the outside catwalk. Richard yelled something that sounded to Vernon like "pumbee." The two men ran through C Module and on down to the lowest working deck on the rig.

Every pipe that required a connection to the sea was on Sixty-eight, as the deck, like the others, was commonly known simply by its height on the rig. Two pumps the size of school buses that sent gas to the rig's generators filled the center of the breezy room. The pumps also injected gas into the transport lines and the ends of the pipelines linking Piper Alpha to Tartan, Claymore, and MCP-01. Coupled to each outgoing and incoming pipeline was a launcher or receiver for pigs, the robot scrubbers sent into the lines to ream out crust and sludge. Sixty-eight was also home to Piper Alpha's resident divers who usually numbered about fifteen. They lived in the accommodation modules like everyone else, but spent their days in the isolation of a separate fiefdom on the west side of the deck. The dive complex included a pair of decompression chambers, a workshop, pump room, two offices, and a photo lab for processing the steady stream of images shot with the divers' helmet cameras. A ladder led to a platform twenty-four feet further down for entering and leaving the sea in a diving bell. On one corner of that platform was a shelter called the Wendy Hut, named after a children's back-yard playhouse common in England, in which divers stayed warm while they waited to go into the water.

Vernon hit the deck on Sixty-eight with Richard right behind him. They ran around the pig stations to the side-by-side A and B injection pumps, both of which were silent except for the hiss of static venting. Vernon saw what looked like lube oil around the base of pump B. That's wrong, he thought. Even with the pumps shut down, the noise on Sixty-eight was loud enough to inhibit conversation. Vernon tapped Richard on the shoulder, pointed over toward the injection pump control board, and yelled, "Restart." Neither man was in a panic. Pump failures were a dime a dozen on an oil rig and both had seen them many times before. At the injection pump control board, Vernon threw a switch to take pump B off-line and clear any electrical glitches. He waited a few seconds, flicked the switch back to run, and pulled the start handle. Nothing. He did it a second time. And a third. Vernon leaned close to Richard, told him to keep trying while he went to the control room to check the maintenance log for Pump A. He had to be absolutely sure the work on the valve had been finished before he tried to start it.

As Vernon trotted back up through C Module to the control room on the mezzanine above D Module, he admitted to himself that he had a serious situation on his hands that was getting worse by the minute. With neither of the injection pumps running, gas flow to the storage tanks that fed Piper Alpha's power generators in D Module had stopped. When the stored gas ran out, the generators were supposed to automatically switch to backup diesel fuel, but that didn't always work. Vernon instinctively reviewed in his mind the steps for a manual diesel fuel restart if the automatic system failed. He'd done it before, but a black start, as the maneuver was called, was the last ditch. Like any factory boss, Vernon hated running out of options. With gas pumps A and B out, Piper Alpha was less than thirty minutes from the most dreaded decision on an oil rig: shut down.

In the main control room upstairs, Vernon's number-two, Geoff Bollands, was even more worried about the rig than his boss. Seconds after he silenced the first alarm and called Richard on the radio, the board lit up again accompanied by a shrill electronic alarm that meant some kind of high-level failure. Bollands quickly discerned the location of the problem: the flash drum, part of the gas distribution system. If the gas plant was crashing, Piper Alpha was headed toward complete loss of power. Even if the backup diesels kicked in, they were only good for an hour, maybe two. If the rig went cold iron with no power at all, the consequences were catastrophic. The oil would stop flowing. Any drills in the ground would stop turning. Everything electrical would fail.

Vernon barged back into the main control room. Bollands told him about the flash drum alarm. Vernon nodded and riffled through the repair and maintenance paperwork on his desk. Pump A was off-line but there was no reason it couldn't be brought to life. Neither Bollands nor Vernon came across any work orders on the pressure safety valve maintenance. They found nothing that changed their minds about trying to restart injection pump A, to which the valve was attached. Vernon filled out the paperwork for bringing pump A back online and called in the maintenance foreman from the next office to add the required second signature to the work order. All that took less than five minutes.

At three minutes to ten, Vernon tore out of the control room and started back to Sixty-eight. On his way down, he passed Erland Grieve, a production tech who had just come on duty when word of the trouble with the pumps rippled around the rig. Vernon told Grieve that both pumps were down. They would give B one more jag then try to start A. By this time, Vernon seemed grim. On Sixty-eight, Richard was at the main control panel ready to reset pump B's system. Vernon took his post at the start handle. Grieve knew that if the gas injection system started, the next step in bringing the generator back online was to restart the local pump, which was controlled by a button on the injection pump housing. He took up his post there. Richard cleared the circuit and hollered at Vernon, who pulled the on handle. They heard the whine of the electric starter motor. Then nothing. Vernon, Richard, and Grieve moved like a choreographed team to the pump A starter panels.

Forty feet above them in the control room, Bollands watched Piper Alpha's gas system shut down. The klaxon alarms for two of the three main compressors in C Module blared and refused to reset when Bollands tried. The third main compressor failed. Bollands was trying to manually switch from the gas generators to the diesels when he heard the high-pitched screech of the special alarms that signaled escaping gas. Every light on the board flashed as the gas alarms automatically shut down other systems. Bollands reached up to engage the diesels.

On Sixty-eight, Bob Vernon, Bobby Richard, and Erland Grieve hit the switches to start condensate injection pump A.

Three

THE DIVERS

On the western edge of Piper Alpha, the divers were oblivious to the confusion on the other side of the rig. Gareth Parry-Davies was fifty feet underwater, sandblasting rust off one of the huge legs. John Barr, in the dive control room on a platform ten feet below Sixty-eight, was tending the air, hot water, and communications umbilical keeping Parry-Davies alive. Two other divers were suited up and waiting in the Wendy Hut. Up on Sixty-eight, one of the divers had just finished an hour in the water working on the Chanter pipeline and was patiently decompressing in one of the two pressure chambers. It was a small cylinder, about fifteen feet long and five feet in diameter, like a punishment cell, with enough room to lie down but not stand up. Along one side was a gray metal bench with a telephone at one end and a narrow bunk lashed to the wall. If a diver did not decompress, he risked pain or death from the bends as gas bubbles inside the body corrupted his joints and tissues. Decompressing in the chamber was better than decompressing in the water by ascending very slowly, but it was still one of the most onerous parts of the job.

In the dive team office a few feet away from the decompression chamber, Piper Alpha's underwater inspection boss Ed Punchard and chief diver Stan McCleod were planning the rest of the night. One of the cranes had moved a heavy piece of the Chanter riser earlier that evening and they'd had to get their divers out of the water, but it had been uneventful from then on. The tides and currents were okay, so they wouldn't lose any time to bad water. Their only problem was that they couldn't find a report confirming that the seawater intakes for the automatic firefighting system would be shut down while their men were in the water. Being sucked into an intake pipe when a pump started unexpectedly was among the grisliest things that could happen to a diver. Punchard and McCleod couldn't take the chance that the guys in the control room had not turned the water system off. They decided to double-check with Occidental's dive rep Barry Barber in the office next door. Barber would either have a copy of the intake report or he would call up to the main control room to confirm the schedule.

On their way out of their own office, Punchard and McCleod stopped to check out their grow-lamp orchard on one of the windowsills. McCleod had brought apple tree seeds and potting soil with him when he came back from shore two weeks earlier. The lamp was left over from somebody's last attempt at oil rig gardening. Anything that eased the hard edges and numbing boredom of life offshore was a welcome touch. As Punchard and McCleod admired the frail green shoots poking through the dirt, a shuddering rumble above them shattered their moment of ease.

Punchard's first thought was that the controllers in C Module had increased the flow of gas to the flare booms again. They had been howling louder than usual since he came on duty that afternoon. Punchard had been on Piper Alpha for five weeks and was leaving in the morning for ten days at home in Cornwall with his wife, Vicky, and their year-old daughter, Susannah. He had come to work three hours ahead of his usual time, hoping to take off early and get a few hours sleep before beginning the trip. Homecoming was always better if he wasn't totally exhausted when he walked in the door. Punchard looked at McCleod and saw that his boss's face showed a puzzled concern that he felt as well. Anything too loud or too hot on an oil rig was serious.

McCleod was a veteran diver from Southampton, England, a big, round-shouldered man in his forties who had gone offshore in the early days, put in his time underwater, stayed alive, and become a dive boss for Stena, the contractor that supplied Piper Alpha's twenty-five resident divers. McCleod gave off a sense of confidence that made him a good leader. He never made any job harder than it had to be, had a steady hand when he was solving problems, and knew that humor was the best way to relax a bunch of tense, tired men. Best of all, he made sure that Occidental Petroleum knew that without his divers to fix their oil rig it would become a rotting tangle of steel in the middle of the ocean in a couple of months. Ed Punchard liked McCleod. He thought Stan was just about what a boss in one of the world's most dangerous places ought to be.

Punchard was thirty-two, a dark-haired, fresh-faced man with the body of a rugby forward and the energy of a twelve-year-old. He was booked on the morning chopper to Dyce, the airport north of Aberdeen, where he would connect with the nonstop to London and a train to Falmouth in southwest England. He loathed and loved helicopters. They were noisy contraptions that glided like a set of car keys if the engines stopped and always seemed to be seconds away from corkscrewing out of control. They were also magic carpets for the ride back to the real world. If disaster struck, they were the only way off an oil rig except for the lifeboats or jumping into the North Sea.

Occidental Petroleum had its own helicopter departure lounge at the Aberdeen airport, across the runway from the passenger terminal for civilians. On his way out to Piper Alpha, Punchard had checked in, had his bags searched, and been issued a heavy neoprene survival suit to wear on the flight. Ten minutes before departure, the lounge agent switched on an overhead television. A video of the procedures for escaping from a helicopter ditching in the sea that everybody had already seen droned overhead. Before a man's first trip offshore, Occidental ran him through three days of training that included the same video and a brutal dunking in a swimming pool in a mock-up chopper to simulate a crash. If you didn't get out quickly enough, they made you do it again. For some guys, the chopper dunk ended their North Sea career before it started.

Nobody in the lounge cared that he could barely hear the soundtrack of the ditching video over the roaring rotors and turbines outside. Muscular, twin-engine Boeing Chinooks and guppy-plump Sikorsky S-61s landed and took off in an endless stream flowing to and from the rigs. At least once a year since the oil boom hit, one of them had crashed or made an emergency landing. More than a hundred men had died in choppers between 1972 and 1985. In

1986, a single, fully loaded Chinook crashed into the sea and killed forty-five more.

Punchard's chopper flight out to Piper Alpha had been typically miserable, but within minutes of takeoff he had switched himself onto offshore time so it didn't matter. Being uncomfortable, working under pressure, and keeping cool was his job. Punchard loved being a diver. One of Punchard's brothers, Bernie, was a commercial diver who lived well and was never out of work. When Ed was in college, Bernie had come within a heartbeat of dying on the job. Punchard had sworn to himself then that he would never follow his brother into his deadly trade no matter how good the money. When another of his brothers talked him into his first scuba dive, his first hour underwater changed everything. The dry suit, weight belt, tank, mask, fins, and snorkel were hot and heavy but Punchard staggered backward into the English Channel and submerged into his future. He saw swarms of spider crabs sidling along a rocky bottom decorated with anemones, urchins, and undulating sea grass. He marveled at the fish that darted right up to his mask and moved so effortlessly in the silent world. He savored weightlessness. The following spring, he enrolled at the Prodive Commercial Diving Center.

Punchard was strong and determined, but the first week at Prodive almost broke him. The day he arrived, expecting some kind of a welcome or an orientation briefing, the instructor in charge of the class of twelve men snapped, "Get on the boat, Mister Punchard." Ed balked. The instructor repeated his command through clenched teeth. "Get. On. The. Boat. Mister. Punchard." They called everybody mister. The instructors shouted every command and ran the place like a military boot camp. Mornings began with an hour of running and a competitive swim in full gear. The man who finished last had to do it again. Punchard, who was just an average swimmer, finished last every day for what seemed to him like an eternity.

Four months later, he was in the best shape of his life, a qualified professional diver, and filled with seething rage for the instructors who had never let up on the misters. After graduation, his tormentors threw a party, called everybody by their first names, and told them why they had been such bastards. "Someday, you may find yourself in the most horrific of situations. The only thing we can do in the course is to apply continuous pressure. If you can't handle that, you won't be able to handle a situation where your life is on the line. It works."

There was no doubt that deepwater oil rig diving was as dangerous a job as a man could do. As one diver put it, "I've got the Rolex watch, the condo in Chamonix, and maybe six months to live." At the end of August 1982, Ed Punchard was ready to go to work. He went north to Aberdeen to look for a job.

The city had calmed down quite a bit during the ten years since the first wave of the oil rush hit in 1972, but it was still a boomtown. Ed lived in his camper on the waterfront and drank in the diver bars at the Imperial Hotel and in a big stone decommissioned church called Gabriel's. Punchard felt good around other divers, except for the ones who flouted their tans and wristwatches. The bars were founts of information for a new diver looking for work. There were six contractors hiring divers out of Aberdeen. Punchard made the rounds every day. He zeroed in on one of them, Comex, which everybody said was the best of the bunch. Eventually, Comex gave him a chance as an air diver on a concrete-leg rig in the Norwegian sector making £50 a day.

The Norwegian job lasted three weeks. He hadn't embarrassed himself underwater, stayed alive, and had enough money to last until whatever came next. By then, he knew that one-time contracts were the bottom of the ladder, even with a good company like Comex. Until he had enough cash to take six months off and pay for the more intensive saturation diving course, the best he could hope for was to land an air-diving spot on one of the big platforms like Ninian Central, Claymore, or Piper that needed divers year-round. After a month of phone calls and sorry-don't-need-any-divers-just-now, Punchard took a three-week pipeline job out of Morecambe Bay on the Irish Sea in Western England.

When that job ended, Punchard went south to Falmouth to take up an invitation from a pretty blonde who said she needed help remodeling her house. Vicky Laloë had been the girlfriend of one of Punchard's classmates in diving school. She was a scuba diver with a quick wit and endless energy. Punchard was sure she was interested even though she was with another guy. One night, after a few beers, she told Punchard that the first time she met him she thought he was a typical arrogant asshole diver. She had changed her mind. He was still arrogant but maybe not an asshole. One night when Punchard was taking the train north, he ran into Vicky in a bar. She told him she had tossed her boyfriend out that day. Whenever Punchard came home, he was welcome to sleep on her floor. Three weeks after he got back to Falmouth, he and Vicky had sanded and painted their way into love remodeling her house. Whatever was next for Ed, he would be coming home to her.

Punchard took another job with Comex and embarked on four years of nomadic diving on rigs owned by BP, Chevron, and Conoco, morphing from baby diver to salty diver. He had almost quit when a decompression chamber on the drilling rig Byford Dolphin exploded, killing five divers. He became a union organizer when he found out that most air divers were making less money than the cooks on the rigs, and wrote a letter to the chairman of Conoco to complain. Under pressure from Conoco, Comex kept Punchard on the Black List until he apologized. Punchard was astounded by how powerful and stupid the oil rig bosses could be. Despite all of it, he didn't object when Vicky decided to take the commercial course at Prodive and look for work offshore herself. They would become the North Sea's first diving couple. The adventure. The headiness of oil rig diving. The money. It was too much to resist. Until it wasn't.

At the end of the year, Ed and Vicky were still a couple when they weren't offshore, but the shine had begun to come off their life together. One night, with Ed in a sullen mood grousing that the oil business was completely out of control and senseless, Vicky slapped a pen and a piece of paper on the table in front of her boyfriend.

"Okay. Enough. We've been spending all our time considering what we've got and trying to make it better. Let's start from what we'd really like. Make a list of three things you'd most like to do and I'll do the same."

Ed wrote: "1. Continue living with Vicky; 2. Work as a marine archaeologist on shipwrecks; 3. Live somewhere nice."

Vicky wrote: "1. Marry Ed; 2. Write books; 3. Live in the sun."

"Right," Vicky said. "We'll start with mine first. Marry me."

"Okay."

"When?"

"Next week."

The following Friday, Ed and Vicky were married at the Falmouth Registry Office. Their first conversation as husband and wife was about item number three on each of their lists. Live in the sun. Live somewhere nice. After a nod to the Seychelles in the Indian Ocean, they settled on the Azores, honeymooned there to reconnoiter, and fell in love with the sleepy Portuguese colony in the Atlantic. Four months later, Vicky was pregnant. They found their dream house in Lagoa on the southern island of the Azores archipelago, a breezy colonial with three stories and a perfect spot on the ground floor for a bistro to generate some cash. They rented the place until they could arrange financing to buy it and moved in. They went back to England for their daughter's birth, returned to the rented house in Lagoa, and in November 1987, their life began to unravel again. The bank turned down their application to refinance the Falmouth house. They needed more money. Vicky couldn't dive with Suzie on her hip, so Ed starting looking for a job offshore.

A few days after Punchard put the word out that he was ready to go back to work, he got a call from a contractor who offered him a three-year deal in Sarawak, Malaysia, that included housing there for his wife and family. It would be the end of their life in the Azores, but he said he would think about it. Before he called Vicky, who was still in Lagoa with Suzie, the phone rang again. It was Stena Offshore. Would Ed be interested in a year's work as the inspection supervisor on Occidental's Piper Alpha? Five weeks on, two weeks off. No diving. He said he was interested, hung up, and called Vicky. She responded to Ed's recitation of the Sarawak and North Sea offers with dead silence. Vicky and Suzie flew home the next day. Before they left Heathrow Airport, they had pronounced the Azores dream dead, decided to take the Piper Alpha offer, and hunkered down to find out what was next for their life together.

A little over three months later, Ed Punchard and Stan McCleod walked from their office on Sixty-eight to the Occidental dive office next door. They found Barry Barber and his clerk, Dick Common, at their desks. Punchard opened his mouth to speak. The lights went out. Shelves flew off the walls. Metal ceiling panels collapsed around him. He felt a withering fear unlike anything he'd ever known. For a few seconds, it felt as though the air had been sucked out of the room and he couldn't breathe. The dive office module was surrounded by a blast shield and the walls remained standing, but the whole rig was shaking violently. In the darkness, Punchard heard Barber scream, "Jesus Christ." McCleod bolted through the door and into the corridor with Punchard right behind him. McCleod yelled over his shoulder, "Find a breathing mask, Ed, and fuck off for your lifeboat."

Before Punchard could leave, a diver materialized in the weird lunar glare of the battery-powered emergency lights that had popped on. "What the hell's going on?" he shouted. "Don't ask me," McCleod snapped. Then, as though coming to his senses and realizing that he was in charge, McCleod spun around to face the diver, grabbed him by the shoulders and said, "What's going on down there? Is everybody okay?"

"I think everybody's okay," Carrol said. "But the door to one of the chambers is blown off and Gareth is still down."

Gareth Parry-Davies was hovering an arm's length away from one of Piper Alpha's massive legs that disappeared below him into the darkness of the deep sea. Oil rig diving wasn't much different from working outside an orbiting spacecraft. Even when performing a task as routine as scrubbing away rust and algae, most rig divers relished the sensations of weightlessness and the pure focus of working in a place as unnatural to human life as the vacuum of space. Kept alive by umbilical cords feeding them air, warmth, and the voice of someone in the real world in the earphones of their helmets, they were alone in a way that normal people rarely knew. It was impossible for a diver to contain the thrill of going to so dangerous a place day after day, impossible to resist the heady truth that he had set himself apart from the ordinary. Most of them eventually tired of the hard labor and risk and took supervisory jobs like Punchard's, but the younger ones were as constantly exhilarated as jet pilots.

At the other end of Parry-Davies's umbilical, John Barr tended him from the dive control room in a gondola suspended ten feet beneath Piper Alpha's sixty-eight-foot level. The twelve-by-fifteen-foot room was as neat and purposeful as NASA's Mission Control, the one place on the rig that never seemed to be patched, broken, or rusty. The lives of the divers depended minute-to-minute on what happened there. Though everyone offshore was exposed to danger of one sort or another, divers were far more likely to die just doing their jobs.

To take care of itself, its wells and pipelines, Piper Alpha was equipped with two diving bells, umbilical reels, and control consoles to monitor two divers in the water at the same time. A row of windows on one wall of Dive Control overlooked the platform from which the divers entered and left the water in the yellow cages of the diving bells. On the facing wall, two color monitors displayed airflow, tool hydraulic pressure, electricity, dive times, suit temperatures, and video feeds from remotely operated television cameras that accompanied divers to record their inspections and repairs. On the panels in front of them, each dive boss could read the flow pressures and contents of tanks outside containing air, oxygen, and helium that were plumbed through Dive Control into the umbilical cords and on to the divers. On the platform outside Dive Control in the Wendy Hut, two divers rested on a bench in full gear, waiting to go to work.

Across a table in the middle of Dive Control, two supervisors' chairs faced each other over communications equipment that linked them to their divers. With only one diver in the water, Barr was alone at the desk. He wore a headset and was holding a one-sided conversation with Parry-Davies, the banter typical of air-dive supervisors who used the voice line to give instructions and simply keep their divers company.

"How about Colchester United last night," Barr said, referring to a loss by Parry-Davies's hometown football team. "It's getting dark up here. Nice night." "Could you possibly work any slower, P-D?"

Parry-Davies, preoccupied with his work, responded with grunts, "Roger that," and "Asshole," but he still received the important message that he was safe and well-tended even though he was working alone underwater.

When Barr's voice wasn't flowing into his helmet, Parry-Davies heard the snap-gurgle of his regulator dispensing air and the clatter of the hydraulic grit gun he was using to scrub the patch of steel in front of him so he could inspect a crack. With the sun gone from the world above, the beam of his helmet lamp splashed the dirty brown leg with a bright yellow light. Like the flame of a campfire, it was enough to see what was right in front of him, but banished everything around him to blackness.

"Forty minutes," Barr said, marking Parry-Davies's down time. He had twenty minutes left before he had to surface.

Four

SILVER PIT

In December 1965, the mobile drilling rig *Sea Gem* had tipped over and vanished into the North Sea, killing fourteen of its thirty-two man crew. Since then, every manned offshore installation in the British sector had to have a standby boat stationed within five miles twenty-four hours a day. It was the law. Public outcry about the new horrors of England's offshore oil fields had forced Parliament's hand over the objections of the oil companies, who had to foot the bill for the standby boats. Those are our men out there, the nation and the newspapers had cried. They aren't mariners. They are far more helpless than men on foundering ships.

Aboard *Silver Pit,* a retired fishing trawler that was Piper Alpha's standby boat, second engineer George Carson meandered up to the galley for his ten o'clock cup of tea. He took a detour out on deck for some air and looked up at the gigantic machine glittering with the last reflections of the sun and its own lights flicking on. It was one of the few times an oil rig could be beautiful. The ocean was calm, a rare condition on the North Sea, triggering in Carson a moment of silent gratitude familiar to all mariners who are freed, however briefly, from bracing themselves against relentless motion. In the winter, a day on a North Sea standby boat was an endurance test even for sailors with the hardiest of sea legs. Some people get nauseated the moment they step on a boat at a dock, but everybody has a threshold beyond which they are plunged into the wretchedness of seasickness. In a winter gale on a notoriously vicious part of the ocean, no one was spared. Calm summer weather was the most precious relief imaginable.

Carson had been all over the North Sea on supply boats before he sat for his engineer's license and began his climb up the maritime officer's ladder with the least desirable engine room job afloat. The pay on an oil rig standby boat was half what other sailors made, and the days at sea were a hundred shades of boring. Even so, Carson had never grown tired of looking at the audacious machines that were out there harvesting the oil.

Silver Pit was four hundred yards northwest of Piper Alpha, jogging in a light southerly with her bow pointing right at the rig. From where he stood on the afterdeck, Carson had to lean over the rail around the wheelhouse to get the full view. Reflecting the twilight, the sooty yellow and gray intruder rising four hundred feet above him was the biggest single thing he had ever seen. The noise of a rig was always a cacophony of roaring turbine exhaust, shrill groans of winch motors, and the clanging of the drill pipes under the derrick. Tonight, it was louder. The flare boom on the southeast corner was spitting a plume hundreds of feet into the air and the stygian howl of the fire drowned out every other sound. Carson shuddered. He hated the thought of being burned, even the sting of a pinched candlewick or the touch of a hot pot on a stove. If fire took control of an oil rig in the middle of the ocean, there was no place for the men to go except into the sea. *Silver Pit,* like the standby vessels on station around every oil rig in the North Sea, gave them a chance.

After *Sea Gem,* even with the hovering standby boats, hundreds of men had died offshore on the North Sea. They had been burned, crushed, and asphyxiated in accidents that are far more common on offshore platforms than in any other kind of heavy industry. They had died in countless helicopter crashes. They had simply vanished when their rigs collapsed and sunk beneath them. The most lethal oil rig disaster in history was the *Alexander L. Kielland,* a semisubmersible rig that failed catastrophically in a gale just after sunset on a March evening in 1980. The *Kielland* was mounted on steel legs over a pair of underwater pontoons, each the size of a navy submarine. The wind and sea were finally lying down after twenty-four hours of hammering the North Sea when one of the main horizontal braces under the rig collapsed. The *Keilland* was on its side in less than a minute and upside down fourteen minutes later. Of the 212 men on the rig, 123 died.

On the deck of *Silver Pit,* George Carson tore his eyes from Piper Alpha and scanned the flat-calm sea around him. That night, a standby boat seemed a bit redundant. Off his starboard side, the massive, twinkling bulk of *Tharos* loomed two hundred yards away. *Tharos* looked like an oil rig, with a helicopter pad, drilling derrick, cranes, and a flare boom, but it was less than a quarter the size of Piper Alpha. It was technically a ship, with its own engines, anchors, twin submerged hulls, and computer-controlled thrusters that could hold its position precisely in most weather. A mile away on the other side of Piper Alpha, the supply ship *Maersk Cutter* was standing by to handle *Tharos*'s anchors, which were so heavy and set so far from the platform that *Tharos* couldn't lift them itself. Much closer to Piper Alpha, the pipeline trenching ship *Lowland Cavalier* lay just twenty-five yards from the rig while her crew and divers worked on the new Chanter riser. Beyond the *Lowland Cavalier,* Carson could see the flare boom and winking lights of Texaco's Tartan platform just above the horizon twelve miles away.

The usual aromas of the sea and the greasy smudge that hovered around an oil rig were overpowered that night by the smell of *Silver Pit*'s red and white five-day-old paint job. She had just had come out of the shipyard in Peterhead after repairs to her fifty-year-old hull and an engine that had seen better days. Since she had been christened *Silver Pit* after the dependable North Sea herring grounds, most of the men who served aboard her referred to the hundred-foot, center-wheelhouse trawler as *The Pit,* but without the derision the nickname implies. Now, *The Pit* was showing her age and the moniker was more apt, but she fulfilled Occidental Petroleum's observance of at least the letter of the law.

Silver Pit had been certified by the British Department of Transport as fit for service as a legal oil field standby vessel for rigs with up to 250 men aboard. The trawler was under the command of John Sabourn, assisted by a mate, chief engineer, second engineer Carson, a cook, and four deckhands who were trained as the crew for *Silver Pit*'s fast rescue craft. The FRC was a rigid-hull inflatable with a diesel water-jet engine that could do thirty knots and hold a dozen people plus its crew of three. Because it had no propellers to snag debris or survivors, it was the best kind of boat for the job. Most offshore sailors called the speedy FRC Z-boats, a reference to the Zodiac inflatables used for rescue operations. When a standby boat was on station around a rig, its Z-boat was always swung from its cradle and hung over the side under its davit, ready to deploy within seconds.

Silver Pit was a clumsy ship, built for the predictable tedium of fishing, with a direct-drive single-screw engine and a small bow thruster useful for docking but not for maneuvering in the open sea. Survivors plucked from the water by the Z-boat would have to climb onto the ship using a rope net hung over the port side amidships, similar to the webbing used by marines during amphibious assaults. *Silver Pit* had no helipad. The only way off except at the dock or alongside a larger vessel was by skiff or in a hoist basket lowered by a hovering chopper. While waiting for evacuation, any survivors would be on their own except for basic first aid.

George Carson was also the ship's medic, a job for which he had taken a two-day class back in Aberdeen so *The Pit* could qualify as a standby vessel. He knew how to splint a simple fracture, how to suture and bandage a minor laceration, and how to administer an injection. About what a Boy Scout earning the first-aid merit badge knew. But even if Carson had been a fully trained physician, there would not be much he could do for a seriously injured man. *Silver Pit*'s small medical chest contained only sterile bandages, iodine, tubes of burn ointment, slings, and tourniquets. There were no saline drips or intravenous needles. Carson had a small personal supply of acetaminophen, an over-the-counter pain medication he was taking for a shoulder injury. There were no other painkillers onboard except for a half dozen syrettes of morphine in a locked box in the master's stateroom. Only the captain, not the medic, could legally administer them.

Carson took a last look at Piper Alpha and walked from the deck into the companionway to the galley. Inside, he looked at the barometer on the bulkhead over the dining table, a sailor's habit that was as instinctive as breathing. The needle was steady, the pressure neither rising nor falling: 29.92. Flat normal. Good. The longer the wind and sea stayed calm the better. He was going to be out there for three and a half more weeks. Next to the barometer, the brass ship's clock ticked over to 2156. Carson glanced at the fruit, bread, cold cuts, and sugar buns on a tray next to the stove but decided to stick to just a cup of tea. Putting on weight at sea was an occupational hazard. The skipper was up in the wheelhouse. Everybody else was in their cabins. Carson put the kettle on and looked out the open porthole over the stove. A light breeze wafted in from the sea as *Silver Pit*'s stern swung a few degrees to put her broadside to the rig that then filled his vision.

For an instant, Piper Alpha was gone. Then it was back. Carson felt rather than heard a gut-rumbling thump and watched an orange and black tongue of flame roll from the production deck. He killed the teapot and ran for the engine room to turn on the hydraulic pumps for launching the FRC. On the bridge, Sabourn had felt the ungodly thud of an explosion and instantly ordered his crew to launch the Z-boat. Its coxswain was a big, forty-year-old veteran sailor named James McNeill. Just four hours earlier, McNeill had arrived onboard to replace a man going home on leave, flying by chopper to *Tharos,* then shuttling to his ship by skiff. He had launched Z-boats countless times in drills, but never before during a real emergency. In two minutes, seamen Charlie Haffey and Andy Kiloh had the orange canvas cover off the boat and McNeill pushed the button on the davit to lower it into the water. McNeill untied the Z-boat's bowline, guided it to the boarding ladder on *Silver Pit*'s lower middle deck, and waited until his two crewmen boarded before following them down. In the Z-boat, McNeill glanced up at Piper Alpha. The tongue of fire he had seen when he came on deck had turned into a glowing ball of flames enveloping the entire side of the rig. Three minutes after the first explosion, McNeill gunned his rescue boat away from *Silver Pit*. For the first time, he felt the heat from Piper Alpha on his face, then noticed how warm he was underneath his bulky neoprene survival suit. Ahead of him, on the lower latticework of the rig, he saw the shadow shapes of men waving frantically toward him.

With the Z-boat launched and headed toward the burning rig,

Sabourn and Carson ran to the bridge to get under way. The closer they could get to Piper Alpha the better. Sabourn ordered ahead slow to the engine room. The deck shuddered, the stack behind the wheelhouse belched a puff of black, and *Silver Pit* started to move. The VHF radio on the bulkhead of the wheelhouse barked.

"Mayday. Mayday. Mayday. All ships. All ships. We have explosion and fire. Explosion and fire."

Carson knew the voice. Piper Alpha's radio operator, David Kinrade, repeated the Mayday for about a minute until the transmission ended in midsentence.

At the Wick offshore communications station on the northern tip of Scotland, the duty officer monitored a weak signal on the long-wave emergency frequency from the oil field to the far northeast.

"This is *Lowland Cavalier, Lowland Cavalier.* We are alongside Piper Alpha . . . alongside Piper Alpha. They have an explosion onboard, an explosion onboard. No numbers of injured or personnel at present. Will update as necessary. Over."

The call from *Lowland Cavalier* was the first of a torrent of Maydays that went on for ten minutes.

At Occidental's pipeline terminal in Flotta on Orkney Island, the night crew were stunned to see the telemetry link to Piper Alpha fail. Minutes later, the oil flow from the rig dropped to zero.

Five

OXY AND THE DOCTOR

On Orkney, lead production operator Lewis Stokan dialed the number for Occidental headquarters in Aberdeen. His call was answered at 10:03 by D. A. Miller, a guard who had just finished his hourly rounds in the four-story Bauhaus pile north of the city from which a hundred people controlled Occidental Petroleum's stake in the North Sea. Stokan told Miller that something strange was going on with the telemetry and oil flow from Piper Alpha. Miller said okay, and made a note in his log. The next call was from the radio operator upstairs at Oxy headquarters. He had just monitored a Mayday from *Tharos*. There had been an explosion aboard Piper Alpha. He didn't know if it was bad or not. Following the Occidental procedure manual, Miller hung up and called the Aberdeen police department. If something bad was happening offshore, the police would alert the emergency crews and equipment on the beach. To be sure that Miller's call was not a hoax, the police duty officer called him right back for authentication. After confirming to the policeman that he had made the first report, Miller pulled out a laminated card and dialed the number at the top of the Occidental executive phone tree. A calm woman's voice with a British accent answered and took his message.

"Please tell Doctor Hammer there is trouble on Piper."

For Armand Hammer, there had always been trouble on Piper Alpha, and it had always been worth whatever it took to fix it. His prize rig was a cash machine that had pumped $25 billion into Occidental's coffers in its fourteen years of existence. It had saved his company from ruin. Hammer had made and lost more fortunes than he could count, but Occidental and Piper Alpha were among his masterpieces as an international tycoon to whom few people in the world could be compared. He even said so himself. "There has never been anyone like me. My likes will never be seen again."

Hammer had just turned ninety. He was a petite five feet, six inches tall, with an owlish countenance that made him seem startled and alert even as an old man. His gray thatch of hair was still parted in the middle as it had been when he was young and sported a black mane slicked back with a light dressing of pomade. His eyes were amber brown and wide-set over a beakish nose and thin-lipped mouth, the left corner of which was always turned up in what appeared to be a perpetual smirk. Most people who did business with Hammer came away with the sensation that they had been observed rather than seen. He was very comfortable with the effects of his presence on others because he had been preternaturally self-aware since childhood.

Hammer was excruciatingly aware of his ancestry, the lore of which colored many of the anecdotes with which he illuminated his stupendous success as a capitalist and oilman. He traced his instincts for conquering adversity to his paternal grandfather, Jacob William Hammer, who inherited from his shipbuilder father a small fortune in salt that was stockpiled on the shore of the Caspian Sea. In 1860, a freak storm destroyed the salt, leaving Jacob Hammer penniless with a wife and two young sons. The ruthless power of divine indifference to Armand Hammer's family next manifested itself when Jacob's wife was trampled to death in a synagogue fire in Odessa, leaving him a widower. Jacob then married Victoria Slepack, the grandmother Armand would know. In Odessa in 1874, their son Julius—Armand Hammer's father—was born. A year later, Jacob Hammer was broke again after his cargo of Polish goose feathers for making quilts arrived covered with mold. He moved his family to America.

Jacob Hammer settled his family near New Haven, Connecticut, on the north shore of Long Island Sound. He eked out a living doing odd jobs for neighbors. Julius, who was fifteen years old, quit school to work in a steel mill. He was a big, ropy laborer who quickly became a champion for the Socialist Labor Party and an organizer of a trade union in the mill. When Julius was nineteen, he persuaded his father to move the family from Connecticut to the Lower East Side of Manhattan. There was no way, Julius insisted, that he could be anything other than a laborer unless he found a profession. Julius's father was bone weary and demoralized by his own lack of success, so he went along with his son's plan and uprooted his family again.

On his first day in New York, Julius Hammer answered an ad from a drugstore in the Bowery that had an opening for a clerk who could speak Italian. The druggist's only question of the obviously Jewish and Russian young man was, "When did you learn to speak Italian?" Julius took a chance that for decades would be part of Armand Hammer's celebration of his genetic boldness in business. "I will learn Italian in two weeks," Julius told the druggist. "If I don't speak it fluently by then, you don't have to pay me anything."

Three years later, Julius owned the drugstore. He also had figured out that most of what he was selling was made from cheap ingredients marked up hundreds of times to generate enormous profits for his suppliers. His obvious trajectory out of the poverty of the Bowery was in the wholesale pharmaceutical business. The young trade unionist took a hard right into capitalism. By the time he was twenty-three, he owned a chain of drugstores in Manhattan and was producing his own brands of nostrums and medicines to stock them. That year, he met and married Rose Lifschitz, a widow with a three-year-old son, Harry. She worked in a garment factory on the Lower East Side. A year later, in their apartment on Cherry Street near the East River, their first son howled into life on May 21, 1898. Though Julius and Rose were in business for themselves, they clung to the enlightened visions of trade unionism and named him Armand: It was an only slightly tongue-in-cheek nod to the symbol of the International Socialist Labor Party, the arm and hammer.

When Armand was four years old, Julius Hammer finished medical school at Columbia College of Physicians and Surgeons and moved his family to the tranquil rural environs of the Bronx. The following year, their second son, Victor, was born, completing what for Armand Hammer would become his inner circle. He witnessed the power of family loyalty as a teenager when Julius hit the skids and declared bankruptcy, accused of hiding assets from his creditors. The lawsuits dragged on for years. The Hammer household, which by then included relatives from Russia who had immigrated to the Bronx, was in a state of siege. Every adult in the family took the witness stand many times. None of them said any more about their finances than "I do not remember," in response to questions from their creditors' lawyers. In fact, when Julius had stopped paying those creditors, he sold his drugstores to his wife's brothers and cousins for next to nothing, maintained control, and kept his medical practice going. The Hammers thrived on the notion that the enemy was all around them and their only allies were blood relatives. Julius Hammer and his family emerged from bankruptcy pretty much unscathed but fiercely radicalized against the capitalist society that had persecuted them with its legal system.

For Armand Hammer, it was only natural that he become a physician so he could work with his father. He enrolled as a premed undergraduate at Columbia and joined the fencing team and Phi Sigma Delta, the only Jewish fraternity on campus. At the beginning of Armand's second year, his father told him that one of his partners wanted to either buy him out or be bought out. Julius had been in business with an accountant named Henry Fingerhood in Good Laboratories, a small factory producing palliatives that were in great demand during the current epidemic of polio. Fingerhood had come to despise Julius Hammer and his financial acrobatics and wanted out. Armand got a $20,000 bank loan, bought out Fingerhood, and went into the drug business, with his father as a shadow partner and cosigner. He paid one of his brightest classmates to take notes for him, skipped lectures, and studied at night. During the day, he ran his company, renamed Allied Drug and Chemical because it sounded more successful than Good Laboratories. Allied Drug was on Third Avenue in Manhattan, with a small store and a workshop in back where two men ran machines making painkillers and two dozen women filled pill bottles. Hammer's business plan was simple: charge less for the pills than the major drug companies and offer doctors samples to encourage them to prescribe them to their patients. It worked. By the time Armand graduated from Columbia with his medical degree, Allied Drug and Chemical had three hundred employees and had moved to a much bigger plant on the Harlem River in the Bronx. Anticipating Prohibition, the Hammer family drug empire added liquor, which could be freely sold for medicinal purposes when prescribed by a physician, to its inventory. By the time he was twenty-two years old, Armand Hammer had made his first million dollars.

While his son prospered in business, Julius Hammer continued to shore up the beachhead of Communism in America. After a bout of intramural doctrinal squabbling, the Socialist Labor Party expelled him, so he jumped to the Left Wing Section of the Socialist Party of the United States, which had direct ties to the Bolsheviks in Russia. Lenin himself noticed the young American doctor who sported a goatee just like his own and seemed tireless in the cause of bringing the Communist message to the workers of the world. The American government noticed Julius Hammer, too, and kept a wary eye on him when he worked out a deal with the Soviet Bureau in Washington, D.C., to export pharmaceuticals and Ford tractors to Russia.

The government surveillance led to suspicions but never resulted in Julius's arrest or deportation for treason. It did rock the Hammer family to its foundation by happenstance. On July 5, 1919, federal agents watched the thirty-three-year-old wife of a former tsarist diplomat enter Hammer's medical office in a wing of the house in the Bronx. Marie Oganesoff, who had accumulated a life-threatening history of miscarriages, abortions, and poor health, was pregnant and wanted to terminate her pregnancy. Six days after the abortion, she died. Four weeks later, a Bronx County grand jury indicted Dr. Julius Hammer for first-degree manslaughter. The following summer, after the prosecutor convinced a jury that Hammer had allowed his patient to "die like a dog" and tried to cover up his crime by attributing Oganesoff's death to influenza, the judge sentenced him to three and a half years in Sing Sing prison.

Armand Hammer took over as the head of his family. He decided to forgo a medical residency to take advantage of the seeds of commerce his father had planted with Lenin and the Bolsheviks while they were still fresh. He was ill-prepared for what he saw when, at twenty-three, he went to Russia to negotiate for the unpaid balance of $150,000 for earlier drug shipments while at the same time prospecting for new trading ventures. The postrevolution famine was catastrophic. Everywhere he went, Hammer saw starving people. He also saw vast supplies of unexploited commodities that would be perfect backhauls aboard ships carrying grain that the Russians so desperately needed. With Lenin's blessing, Hammer made a deal to deliver 36 million pounds of flour in return for exclusive concessions to export asbestos, art, furs, leather, hair, sausages, jade, caviar, lace, rubber, and cigarettes. The American government was uneasy about young Dr. Hammer's connections in Russia, but accorded him the status of a diplomat for back-channel communications with the enemy.

By the time Armand Hammer took a flyer on a little oil company in California thirty-five years later in 1956, he had decorated his office walls with photographs of himself with kings, presidents, dictators, and movie stars. He was an icon of global capitalism. He made money in mining, pencils, typewriter parts, stationery, wheat, beer, whiskey, and bull semen. He was revered as a philanthropist whose gifts to cancer research and education were celebrated all over the world. With his brother, Victor, he had gone into the art business in New York, London, and Paris, and systematically assembled the world's greatest collection of Impressionist and Post-Impressionist paintings, which he installed in a new museum bearing his name in Los Angeles. The doctor lived nowhere and everywhere, with homes in several cities, a headquarters in Los Angeles, and a succession of private planes aboard which he spent much of his time. He and his lawyers were never far away from the courtrooms in which Hammer was constantly being sued. From the time of his father's bankruptcy, not a day had passed when the name Hammer was not on a piece of paper in an active legal proceeding somewhere. He treated the endless judicial combat as a natural part of doing business, unabashedly telling the world that "Those who insist on telling the truth never have a future. The only way to build the future is to build it on lies."

Hammer didn't exactly lie to his partners on the North Sea, but he didn't tell them that his company would go bankrupt unless Piper Alpha became the most productive oil platform in history. Against those odds, most of them would have placed their bets with another oil company. The phone call that there was trouble on the Piper meant that everything Hammer owned was on the line. There was no state in which he was happier. He loved repeating what the circus aerialist Karl Wallenda said about danger: "Life is on the wire. The rest is waiting."

When Armand Hammer congratulated himself on his success, as he often did, he said, "A businessman has to have a love affair with money, and money happens to be my first, last, and only love. That's why I'm so brilliant at what I do." Despite his monogamous relationship with money, Hammer had countless lovers and married three times. His first wife was a Russian actress named Olga Van Root, with whom he had his only child, Julian. Hammer divorced Olga in 1943 to marry Angela Zeveley, an opera singer whose career had been ended by an automobile accident that impaired her hearing. His third wife, Frances Tolman, who had plenty of money after the death of her first rich husband, became Hammer's partner in a tax-shelter loan to Occidental Petroleum, a decrepit corporation traded on the Los Angeles Oil Exchange.

Occidental had done little to distinguish itself since its founding by a California wildcatter in 1920. It seemed amazing to Hammer that it could still be in business, though he did not understand the precipice upon which most oil exploration companies routinely stood. In 1956, Occidental had reported assets of just $79,000, which included some oil field hardware and the rights to drill a pair of new wells, one in Fresno and the other near San Jose. The company was a perfect tax shelter for the Hammers, whose loans of $50,000 each could be written off in a single year, and might give them a share in a bonanza if the new wells struck oil without exposing them as owners of Occidental Petroleum. The wells came in four months after they wrote their checks, and Armand and Frances Hammer fell head over heels in love with the oil business. They bought a mobile home and camped out at their wells listening to Gene Autry records, hanging out with the roustabouts, and savoring the raw aromas of crude oil that perfumed the air. For the first time in Hammer's life, his precious money had a smell.

Even with the success of Fresno and San Jose, and the enchantment of crude oil, the Hammers still had no interest in becoming the owners of an oil company. The following year, they loaned Occidental $112,000 so it could acquire drilling rights to a tract in the Los Angeles suburb of Dominguez Hills. The owner of the Dominguez field was a Texas wildcatter named J. K. Wadley who needed some money and couldn't wait for it while he drilled the wells. As Occidental's most famous negotiator, Hammer made the deal himself, offering Wadley $1 million in cash with another $750,000 payable in eighteen months. Wadley took the money, but couldn't shake the feeling that the intense little man who bought his wells had put one over on him with nothing but charm.

The Dominguez field came in big and turned Occidental into a legitimate though minor player in the big game dominated by the Seven Sisters: Standard Oil of New Jersey, Standard Oil of New York, Standard Oil of California, Texaco, Gulf, Shell, and British Petroleum. Hammer was sure he could make a fortune in oil that would dwarf everything he had made until then. He also knew that drilling for oil and pumping money from the earth would be more fun than he had ever had in his life. So he took an ownership position in Occidental Petroleum.

With his stake in Occidental, Armand Hammer joined a long line of petroleum buccaneers that began in the summer of 1859 when an out-of-work railway express agent named Edwin L. Drake got lucky in a muddy field in Titusville, Pennsylvania. Drake had been hired by a group of New England investors to prove a theory that the thick, black rock oil that seeped from springs could be pumped from the ground in the same way as water. Rock oil was already being sold as a patent medicine to relieve headaches, toothaches, deafness, stomach upset, worms, rheumatism, and dropsy (edema), and to heal wounds on animals. The dominant brand of this panacea was Seneca Oil, named in honor of Chief Red Jacket, who had passed on the curative secrets of oil to white men. One of the purveyors of Seneca Oil included in his advertising a poem about its healing power.

The Healthful balm, from Nature's secret spring,
The bloom of health, and life, to man will bring;
As from her depths the magic liquid flows,
To calm our sufferings and assuage our woes.

A view of Aberdeen harbor
(Courtesy of the author)

Piper Alpha
(From the Cullen Report, UK Department of Energy)

Piper Alpha and *Tharos*
(Press Association)

A typical North Sea oil rig stateroom
(Courtesy of the author)

Piper Alpha minutes after the outbreak of the first fire
around 10:00 p.m., July 6, 1988

(From the Cullen Report, UK Department of Energy)

Piper Alpha after the rupture of the Tartan pipeline, around 10:22 p.m.

(From the Cullen Report, UK Department of Energy)

The *Silver Pit* in Aberdeen harbor
(Aberdeen Press and Journal)

Fast rescue craft (Z-boat)
(From the Cullen Report, UK Department of Energy)

The remains of Piper Alpha on July 7, 1988
(Press Association)

Red Adair fighting the still-burning blaze on Piper Alpha, July 10, 1988
(Press Association)

Piper Alpha's Accommodation Module A on the wharf
at Flotta, after its recovery from the sea
(Aberdeen Press and Journal)

Occidental Petroleum
president and majority
shareholder
Armand Hammer
(Aberdeen Press and Journal)

Lord William Douglas Cullen
(Aberdeen Press and Journal)

Piper Alpha survivor Bob Ballantyne
(Aberdeen Press and Journal)

Ann Gillanders (left) with Bill Barron and wife, Trish, at the
Piper Alpha Families and Survivors Association office in Aberdeen, 1990
(Aberdeen Press and Journal)

Ed Punchard as a young diver
(Courtesy of Ed Punchard)

Piper Alpha memorial, Aberdeen
(Courtesy of the author)

Sperm whale oil had been the standard for high-quality, low-smoke illumination for centuries but it was becoming scarce because whalers had killed most of the whales already. Finding a replacement for whale oil was the holy grail for hucksters and inventors. Anybody who could banish the night with new light when all the whales were dead would make the greatest fortune the world had ever seen. A few tried camphene, made from turpentine harvested from pine trees, which produced good light but had the dangerous properties of a high explosive. What was called town gas could be distilled from coal and piped into homes, but it was expensive and available only in big cities. A Canadian geologist had patented a way to refine lamp oil from asphalt and tar pits, and named it kerosene, from the Greek words *keros* and *elaion,* which mean "wax" and "oil." By 1859, when Drake trundled into Pennsylvania, kerosene production was a $5 million industry in the United States. The only problem was finding enough tar, asphalt, or crude oil. Drilling might be the answer.

With a blacksmith named Uncle Billy Smith, Drake started drilling a well more than a hundred feet deep into the Pennsylvania shale. Over and over, their equipment snapped off in the ground or stuck fast or just wouldn't work. Drake's well was a hole in the ground into which money flowed and nothing came out. In mid-August, his investors ran out of patience. They wrote a letter telling Drake to pay the final bills, pack up, and come home to Connecticut.

Late in the day on August 27, while the letter ending the venture was still in the mail, Uncle Billy's drill was at sixty-nine feet and still turning. The pipe lurched, dropped six inches into what the men above assumed was some kind of subterranean cavern, and stopped. Enough for today, Drake said. He sent his men to their tents for the night and told them he'd be back on Monday. The next morning, Sunday, Uncle Billy strolled out to the derrick, peered down the drill pipe, and saw a dark fluid floating on top of the hole. Using a tin rain spout, he drew off some of the heavy, brownish liquid, smelled it, and knew that he had tapped an underground pool of the same stuff that oozed out of the local springs.

Six years later, oil derricks were more common than windmills in western Pennsylvania, New York, and Ohio. Investors rushed to build refineries to distill the crude into fine lamp oil and, increasingly, lubricants for the machinery of modern manufacturing. The boom almost fell apart because nobody really knew how to handle great quantities of oil or even what to put it in. They used forty-gallon wooden whiskey barrels first, simply because they were ready-made. Five years after Drake's discovery, oilmen standardized for the international trade with specially built forty-two-gallon barrels that were closer to the old English wine measurement, the tierce.

Despite insatiable demand and apparently endless supplies, the oil business was chaotic. In the winter of 1865, two men who owned a kerosene refinery in Cleveland met to resolve a bitter disagreement about how fast their company should expand. Maurice Clark wanted to move slowly. His partner, John D. Rockefeller, had a vision of owning not only refineries but oil fields, railroads, trucking lines, and lamp oil distributorships all over the country, thus removing chaos from the oil business. At an impasse, Clark and Rockefeller decided that one of them should buy the company from the other in a private auction to be held immediately. They started at $500. Five minutes later, Clark bid $72,000. Rockefeller countered with $72,500. Clark said the hell with it. Standard Oil is yours, John.

Rockefeller threw himself wholeheartedly into what he called the Great Game, driven to make money for its own sake and as a gauge of his personal achievement. He poured his profits into the Cleveland refinery, built another one, and set up a trading company in New York to manage Atlantic Coast markets and expand into Europe. By the end of the 1870s, Rockefeller had a global monopoly in the market for the "new light," and Standard Oil was the first multinational corporation.

Rockefeller and the American oilmen had the business all to themselves through the illumination era and well into the modern iterations of petroleum consumption for propulsion, lubrication, and molecular hydrocarbon engineering. The British joined the Americans to open up Iran and the rest of the Middle East to oil production. The Russians, with American, British, and Dutch partners, developed vast fields in the Caspian and the far east. Oil was everywhere. The demand was insatiable. Rockefeller's Great

Game had created not only a new kind of global corporation but had transformed the concept of limitations in the evolution of a trading market. The population of the earth doubled from the end of World War II to the mid-sixties, and petroleum consumption kept pace. The vagaries of the market seemed to even out with the sheer application of the invisible hand of capitalism. Gasoline for the world's blooming love affair with automobiles and airplanes was cheap.

Driven by demand, the technology for hydrocarbon extraction evolved, too, enabling oil and gas production from deposits under water, ice, and the shifting sands of deserts. No place on the planet was immune to the quest for petroleum. The optimism about our apparently limitless oil resources paled a bit when Arab countries in the Middle East, Mexico, and Venezuela nationalized their oil fields. With a stroke of a pen, they simply seized the wells, equipment, and everything else the foreign corporations had implanted on their soil. Then, with the emergence of the Organization of Petroleum Exporting Countries (OPEC), petroleum became a weapon that could put pressure on cultural, religious, or military opponents. The threat to commercial order from politically manipulated oil prices was compounded by the threat to the security of wealthy nations. Since World War I, when First Lord of the Admiralty Winston Churchill began fueling his battleships with heavy bunker oil instead of coal, petroleum had been a strategic commodity. During the next war, Churchill and his allies built PLUTO (Pipe Line Under The Ocean), the world's first underwater pipeline across the English Channel, to keep their tanks and trucks moving during the invasion of France. Oil was more critical to warfare than bombs.

A hundred years after Drake's well, succeeding in the oil business required people who could charm and manipulate international diplomats as well as cutthroat corporate masterminds. No one was more perfectly suited for the job than Armand Hammer. He had already amassed one of the world's great fortunes. Through his philanthropy, art collection, and fame, he had achieved equal footing with enough heads of state that they did not intimidate him. Eight years after making his first loans to Occidental, Hammer was the corporation's president and chairman of the board. Annual sales were $600 million after major oil and gas discoveries in Texas, Oklahoma, Kansas, and Colorado. Hammer and his wife owned 40 percent of Occidental stock, which was listed on the Big Board of the New York Stock Exchange as OXY. Despite protests from the Occidental board of directors, Hammer risked it all in the North African desert.

In 1965, Hammer slipped his nose under the tent of the emerging North African oil fields in Libya, challenging the Seven Sisters in a competition for the rights to drill into what most geologists believed might be the greatest petroleum deposits ever found. Sayyid Muhammad Idris al-Mahdi al-Sanusi, the first and only king of the formerly nomadic tribes of Libya, had come up with a new way to award concessions for oil drilling in his kingdom. Instead of granting exclusivity to a single corporation or consortium as had been the custom in the past, King Idris divided Libya into eighty-four separate parcels on which anyone could bid. When word of Idris's plan filtered through the international oil community, everybody understood that he had come up with the perfect plan to maximize licensing fees, royalties, and bribes for the royal family. The Seven Sisters hated the Libyan plan. Armand Hammer loved it.

The doctor arrived in Libya's capital, Tripoli, aboard a chartered plane to present Occidental's bid to King Idris, who met him at the airport. Idris remarked that the French Dassault Falcon jet was one of the most beautiful planes he had ever seen. Hammer called the charter company, bought the jet, and gave it to Idris on the spot. The king offered perfunctory objections, but accepted the gift. At the palace, Hammer presented Idris with a solid gold chess set and got down to business. The Occidental bid, one of 120 that the king would receive, immediately stood out from the others. It was leather-bound, with a cover-label of handwritten sheepskin parchment, wrapped in red, black, and green ribbons, the colors of the Libyan flag. Inside the stunning package, Idris found not only numbers but a detailed plan for an experimental farm at an oasis where Idris's father was buried. Three months earlier, Hammer had bought out the International Ore and Fertilizer company, which would oversee the farm and give fertilizer to the perennially crop-poor farmers of Libya. Occidental would also build an ammonia plant and food preservation warehouses to further support Libyan agriculture. Privately, Hammer whispered to the king that he had set up individual bank accounts in Switzerland for members of the royal family into which monthly payments would flow as long as Occidental was in Libya.

In February 1966, King Idris awarded Occidental two of the most potentially valuable concessions to drill in Libya, in return for a one-eighth royalty to the government for any discovery, plus a 50 percent tax on profits. Hammer signed the contracts in March and sent his drillers into the desert to look for the oil that the geologists told him was there. Over the next six months, he spent $3 million on seismic testing and $1 million each for three wells drilled to depths of ten thousand feet that produced nothing but sand. Occidental directors and stockholders joked about "Hammer's Folly" and plotted to overthrow their president and chairman, who continued to insist that his geologists were right. In November 1966, as real action against Hammer by his board was beginning to take shape, Occidental drillers using the most up-to-date technology to explore in several directions from a single well hole struck oil. A month later, they did it again. It was light sweet crude, the best kind, with low sulfur content that burned clean. If the early flows were accurate measures of the reserves in the Occidental tracts, the company was sitting on three billion barrels of recoverable crude. When Hammer announced the bonanza to a gathering of a thousand stockholders in a Los Angeles hotel ballroom, he compared himself to Edwin Drake and his nick-of-time reprieve from failure. One of his directors quipped that Drake and now Hammer had just gotten lucky at the right moment. Hammer smiled at the man. "Let me tell you weak sisters how to spell luck in the oil business," Hammer snapped. "G-o-o-d g-e-o-l-o-g-i-s-t-s."

Finding the oil was one thing. Getting it to market from the middle of the Libyan desert was another. Every petroleum engineer Hammer talked to said it would take at least three years to build a pipeline 150 miles to tidewater, by which time Occidental would be a bankrupt memory. Hammer tried to make a deal with Esso for a joint venture on a pipeline the oil giant was already building, but Esso wanted no part of the doctor. With a single bold stroke, Occi-

dental had become a force to be reckoned with as the fourth largest
oil company in terms of the reserves it controlled. In early 1967,
Hammer had no choice but to go it alone on the pipeline or lose
Occidental. In a last ditch maneuver, he went to Stephen Bechtel,
head of the eponymous international construction company that
had been building pipelines in Libya for five years. With nothing
but promises of future Occidental contracts and the force of his personality, Hammer convinced Bechtel to build the pipeline on credit
and to do it in not three years but one year.

The push to complete the pipeline imposed inhuman demands on
the thousands of foreign and Arab workers who built it. Hammer
ordered the work to proceed around the clock. The temperature
in the desert reached 120 degrees during the day. The men strung
lights to work through the night. There were so many injuries and
deaths that Bechtel field boss John McGuire blew the whistle and
testified before the United States Senate on the horrendous conditions on the Occidental job in Libya. "The desert heat did get to the
brain. Some grown men came up to me and cried at my feet, begging me to let them leave the country. When Arab laborers would
get down on their knees and pray to Mecca six times a day, the
Occidental-Bechtel people were crawling all over them. There was
absolutely no adherence to safety standards of any kind."

The first oil flowed through Occidental's pipeline in February
1968, fifteen months after Bechtel's construction army went to work.
Armand Hammer's Libyan oil coup catapulted him to the front
rank of the world's oil tycoons. In six months, the price of Occidental stock doubled. In September 1969, when Hammer was riding a
wave of fame and unimagined wealth, twenty-seven-year-old Libyan colonel Muammar el-Qaddafi deposed King Idris in a bloodless
revolution. As president of the Libyan Arab Republic, Qaddafi canceled all concessions granted by King Idris. The oil companies had
to submit new bids acceptable to him or face the possibility of losing
everything if he nationalized the oil fields, which was a possibility.
Armand Hammer's first move after he heard about the coup was to
cancel the monthly Swiss bank payoffs to King Idris and his family.
After a year of tense negotiations with Qaddafi, Hammer held on to
his wells in the desert, but at a much higher price in fees, royalties,

and bribes that left Occidental in ruins. Hammer vowed to never again risk drilling for oil in an unstable country. To resuscitate his crippled company, the doctor threw everything he had into negotiations with the safe, sensible government of Great Britain and bet his company on the North Sea.

Six

PIPER ALPHA

Fifteen years later, Bobby Richard on Piper Alpha pushed the starter button on condensate injection pump A. In the split second before he could pull his hand back from the instrument panel, a globe of dark orange flame swept across the deck and enveloped him in hellish fire. Bob Vernon was around the corner from Richard, partially shielded by the pump itself. The blast knocked Vernon senseless. His face and hands were burned, but he was alive. Erland Grieve, too, was lucky, insulated from the blast by the full bulk of one of the big pumps. As quickly as it had materialized, the rolling fire disappeared, leaving a wake of suffocating heat and the crackling of the fuel oil fires it had ignited around the machinery. The ceiling was trembling. Vernon and Grieve bolted up the ladder toward the main control room in D Module, Vernon shouting that he had to be sure the firefighting water pumps were switched on manually. When he had come on duty, he had noted that the automatic system was off because there were divers in the water.

In the main control room twenty feet above the explosion, Geoff Bollands and his assistant, Alex Clark, flew off their feet and slammed into the wall. Both men were conscious. Bollands had a deep gash in his left hand and the pain kept him on the floor. Clark had hit the wall headfirst. He was covered with blood from cuts on his face but rose to his knees through a waist-high haze of putrid smoke that filled the room. The control panels were a mess of broken glass and sparking electrical wires. Telephones and radio mikes swung on their cords. Clark looked down through the smoke and saw Bollands writhing on the floor, but the screech of metal-to-metal torment made saying anything to him impossible. Pushing the emergency button to shut down Piper Alpha was Bollands's call as the lead production man in the control room. Clark could see that his friend was in no condition to make it. He dropped to the floor, crawled on his elbows and knees to what was left of the control panel, reached up through the suffocating smoke, and hammered the button. Nothing changed. Clark covered his eyes with the crook of his arm, reached down, and pulled Bollands to his feet. Together, the men staggered to the door. Their lifeboat stations were thirty feet away.

In the corridor, they ran into Vernon and Grieve. Vernon shouted, "Are the fire pumps on?" Still dazed, neither Bollands nor Clark could give him an answer. Vernon went around the corner to look for an emergency breathing apparatus. The smoke on the production deck was so thick by then that there was no chance of reaching the fire pump controls in D Module without one. Piper Alpha's safety chief, Bob Carroll, ran into the corridor and asked the same question about the pumps. He smashed the glass on the manual alarm set into the corridor bulkhead, which should have set off a deluge from overhead spray valves. Nothing happened. Vernon ran back to the men clustered in front of the control room door. He had two breathing tanks and handed one of them to Carroll without a word. Tucking the tanks under their arms, holding their masks to their faces, Vernon and Carroll took three steps into the control room and disappeared into sooty darkness lit only by crackling electrical arcs.

Meanwhile, forty feet higher on the rig in Piper Alpha's cinema, Bill Barron was drifting in and out of *Caddyshack* when the screen collapsed to the floor. The images stuttered, then disappeared into accordion folds. The ordinary vibrations of the rig took on the intensity of a lurching ship. What sounded like a car slamming on its brakes and skidding drowned out the still-running soundtrack of the movie. Barron shook himself fully awake, stood, and trotted up the aisle feeling not so much fear but curiosity. He got to the door right behind Michael Jennings, who had been sitting in the back of the room. Jennings was the fight logistics officer, the man in charge of Piper Alpha's helicopter pad. With a knot of men shuffling behind them, they opened the door into the central corridor of C Deck in the accommodation module. There was no panic. Everybody had been through at least one frightening moment offshore. Hours of drills had conditioned them to respond rather than react to explosions, fire, and gas leaks so they would have the best possible odds for survival. Some of them had been aboard four years earlier when an explosion had forced evacuation of the rig. There were injuries, but choppers had shuttled from *Tharos* to the helideck at the top of Piper Alpha and gotten everybody off alive. Their instructions were to muster in the canteen or at their lifeboat stations and wait for instructions. For most of the men, there was no choice but to follow orders and prepare for evacuation, their moods buoyed by the possibility that they would be in Aberdeen that night.

Seven

THE GRANITE CITY

For half a century, the tongue of the ocean shared by England, Scotland, Scandinavia, and Northern Europe tantalized oilmen after they drilled productive wells in the Dutch lowlands. Geologists knew that the petroleum-bearing strata of Holland extended into the North Sea, but offshore test wells had produced only minuscule quantities of oil and gas. Part of the cause for this lack of success was the availability of cheap crude in the United States, the Middle East, and South America, which reduced the need to take the risks of drilling in deep water. When some of the petroleum-rich nations began using oil as a weapon, Rockefeller's Great Game changed forever.

In 1951, Iran threw out the British Anglo-Iranian Oil Company and nationalized the fields upon which the Western powers had been depending for twenty years. Five years later, Egypt seized the Suez Canal and began a war with England, France, and Israel for control of the vital energy seaway. The big ditch through the desert connecting the Red Sea and the Mediterranean had been under British and French rule for seventy-five years, shortening by six thousand miles the voyage that petroleum from the Middle East had to travel to markets in energy hungry Europe and North America. After Egypt took control, the Suez was closed for the year that it took to clear shipwrecks, some of them sunk intentionally to stem the flow of oil during the war. Diplomacy, United Nations Peacekeeping Forces, and the pragmatism of global commerce reopened the Suez. Even with the Middle East in business again, petroleum-importing nations, including the United States, France, and England, began

frantic campaigns for energy independence. They started building
fast tankers that didn't need canals to get their product to market. In the mid-sixties, oil in Alaska, the Gulf of Mexico, and the
North Sea that had been too expensive to extract started to look
like a bargain.

Drilling for oil on the bottom of the ocean began in 1896 when a
desperate wildcatter who had been shut out of the action on land in
Southern California punched a shallow well at the end of a pier in
Santa Barbara. His little pipe produced only two barrels of crude a
day but it was the first oil well in saltwater. The rush that had begun
in Titusville, Pennsylvania, forty years earlier had finally made its
way into the seven-eighths of the planet dominated by water. By the
1920s, stilt-legged platforms sprouted in Santa Barbara Channel;
Lake Maracaibo, in Venezuela; and coastal lakes of Louisiana, but
these were pumping oil in water almost shallow enough for wading.
Everybody in the oil business knew that the future was in the deep
ocean where prospectors were finding the same geologic formations
that yielded outrageous gushers on land.

On a clear Sunday morning in October 1947, drillers working
for the pioneer oil syndicate Kerr-McGee put the puzzle together
and struck oil ten and a half miles off the Louisiana coast. The
Kerr-McGee exploration rig was just a big power barge with a derrick mounted over a hole cut in the bottom, but it proved it could be
done. The technology of offshore drilling and production exploded.
Drilling rigs were mounted on ships, barges, fixed platforms made
of steel and concrete, platforms with submersible pontoons, and
floating platforms held in place by cables anchored to the bottom.
The oilmen sunk wells ten thousand feet and more into the seafloor.
They figured out how to bore not only straight down but in several
directions with a single drill head.

In 1962, a Phillips Petroleum vice president on vacation in Holland had toured a drilling derrick near Groningen and decided the
time was right for systematic exploration of the North Sea. Two
years later, he and the other top executives left the boardroom at
Phillips headquarters in Bartlesville, Oklahoma, and spent a day

crawling around on the company's basketball court looking at three hundred feet of seismic data from what he knew would become the Norwegian sector. They already knew that the Norwegians would want a huge share of whatever they found in return for drilling rights, but if the seismic tracings on the basketball court were right, there was plenty of oil to make a lot of people very rich and free a lot of nations from dependency on imported petroleum. Five years later, the Phillips Petroleum–chartered drilling rig *Ocean Viking* punched thirty-two very expensive dry holes in water three hundred feet deep to subterranean depths of ten thousand feet. In November 1969, Phillips headquarters reluctantly telexed their office in Norway. Don't drill any more wells. Their production chief wrote back that he had already paid for the *Ocean Viking* through the spring of the following year. He didn't think he could find anybody to sublease it. The weather was terrible, but why not drill one last well. The home office said okay. Drill. On a fishing bank known as Ekofisk two hundred miles southwest of Stavanger, under two hundred feet of water and ten thousand feet of rock, *Ocean Viking*'s drill bit into a billion-barrel reservoir of light sweet crude. It was an Elephant.

British Petroleum—the renamed and partially nationalized Anglo-Iranian Oil Company—ordered its exploration rig *Sea Quest* into a tract a hundred miles northwest of Ekofisk that had been known to fishermen for centuries as the Long Forties. The sprawling underwater plain got its name from its uniform depth of forty fathoms, or 240 feet. Until then, no producing oil wells had ever been drilled in water so deep. In October 1970, British Petroleum found a lake of oil underneath the North Sea. The following summer, after drilling through a winter of howling gales and fifty-foot seas, Shell found a third Elephant in the far north. Shell spent two months confirming the unbelievable proportions of its discovery in secrecy that rivaled the D-Day invasion of Europe. It was larger than Ekofisk and Forties, with two billion barrels of recoverable crude, four trillion cubic feet of gas in a layer of rock three thousand feet thick that began seven thousand feet beneath the surface in 450 feet of water.

The stakes on the North Sea were enormous. Britain had already opened the auction for its fourth round of licensing. Shell wanted

Brent and the surrounding tracts with the same geologic signatures
all to itself. A hundred miles southwest of Brent, seismic testing and
core samples hinted at the existence of another field that might be
as big as Ekofisk, Forties, and Brent. The oil survey maps labeled
it Piper, after the rock formation in which it was found. Armand
Hammer booked suites in the posh Claridge Hotel in London and
went to work on his contacts at Downing Street and Windsor Cas-
tle. Shell could have Brent. He wanted Piper.

A month after the revelation of the Brent Elephant, the extraction
of North Sea oil was one of the most attractive investments in the
world, a new twist in a volatile business that had been crippling corporations and financiers for a hundred years. It promised a friendly
stable government and the logistical conveniences of an industrially
developed nation. Three cities on the northeast coast of Scotland had
harbors and railheads that could handle decades of occupation by
armies of people and equipment. Peterhead, Aberdeen, and Dundee.
For two years, the oil companies played the cities against each other,
promising a flood of jobs in return for land on the waterfront, tax
breaks, and relief from the demands of the trade unions. The city
that promised the most would become the oil capital of Europe.
Each was desperate to rejuvenate itself and find some way to hold
on to its young people who were fleeing the miseries of adulthood
with no way to make a decent living. Ten years of the Scottish Plan
to rebuild the economy had produced a total of three hundred jobs
in three new companies, a carbon paper manufacturer, a Michelin
wheel rim plant, and a firm of bespoke tailors. The fishing fleets
still went to sea and delivered cod, haddock, sole, and mackerel
to fish markets, but industrial factory trawlers had decimated the
stocks. Young men in once-prosperous fishing families needed jobs
as badly as everyone else. There was some big, old money in Northeast Scotland, but its custodians, generations removed from the
enterprise and ambition that had created the wealth, were cycling
very little of it through the economy. The politicians and business
leaders of Dundee, Aberdeen, and Peterhead came like supplicants to
the bargaining table with the oil companies. Peterhead was the first
loser. The city had a breakwater harbor, but no airport. It would be
perfect for relocating what was left of the fishing fleets of Northeast

Scotland, but not for the kind of logistics the oilmen had in mind. Dundee faded out of the picture when waterfront unions made it clear that they were going to maintain their hold on every scrap of material that crossed the city's docks. Aberdeen had a small but serviceable harbor, decent near-shore anchorages, a former Royal Air Force base with runways long enough to land jets, and civic leaders who were clamoring to sell or lease vital land to the oil companies. By 1972, the executives at Shell, British Petroleum, Texaco, Occidental, and Phillips had anointed the quiet market town on the edge of the Highlands as the Scottish Klondike.

For centuries, Aberdeen had nourished a stable population of farmers, fishermen, whalers, cattlemen, and miners who had dug the largest man-made hole in Europe, the five-hundred-foot-deep open pit of the Rubislaw quarry. Aberdeen's buildings are predominantly stone, many of its streets cobbled, the steep hillside sloping to the sea still part of the urban topography. Looking down the mile-long straightaway of Union Street was like gazing through a stone canyon. The houses, pubs, churches, storefronts, and the street itself were granite, a particular kind of local rock infused with chips of mica that gave the city a silvery sheen. Every summer, as though an intentional counterpoint to the harsh surfaces of all that granite, roses in hundreds of perfectly tended formal gardens bloomed to perfume Aberdeen. In stores, on buses, at work, people talked about the roses like most people talk about a streak of lovely weather.

Compared with the industrial muscle of Glasgow and the aristocratic solidity of Edinburgh, Aberdeen was a prim, reclusive member of the family of ancient Scottish towns. It was a city of well-heeled complacency that time and again had opted out of the opportunities for dramatic expansion, a city of rich tea planters' spinster daughters living off safe investments, and workaday people who lived and were gone. Aberdonians evolved their own language, a throaty brogue known as Doric, which is indecipherable to outsiders. Aberdeen's citizens had more savings accounts than those of any other Scottish city, fed by men and women who quietly feasted off tourism and service industries. It also had a core of lawyers, bankers, insurance agents, tradesmen, merchants, and enough low-paid laborers to keep things moving. People called it the Cosy Corner, trusting it to remain the same while everything else was changing.

Beneath the settled routines of the Cosy Corner, Aberdeen was hiding a moribund economy. During the first half of the twentieth century, granite quarries, paper factories, fishing fleets, sheep, cattle, and textile mills established Aberdeen as the third largest city in Scotland, the center of commerce for the northeast corner of the British Isles. By the early 1960s, the *Economist* magazine characterized the city as a community in a stupefying torpor that masked steady decline. No significant new employer had set up shop in Aberdeen since World War II because of a notable reluctance to make newcomers welcome. The president of the city's chamber of commerce was quoted in the article: "Let industry come to Northeast Scotland. Just not here." The announcement of the closing of the Rubislaw granite quarry appeared in the same edition of the Aberdeen *Press and Journal* as the news of Phillips Petroleum's Ekofisk discovery. Many Aberdonians later interpreted the coincidence as an omen.

Just before the oil arrived, the two hundred thousand people living in Aberdeen had organized themselves as a large rural service town rather than an urban center straining to grow. Local commerce evolved along the two main thoroughfares, Union and George streets, with a hundred and twenty-five bars, thirty-four hotels, thirteen movie theaters, four bingo clubs, three gambling casinos, eighty-four betting shops, and fifty-five social clubs. Aberdeen was on the circuit for annual visits by the national ballet, orchestra, and opera companies. The crime rate in the city was surprisingly low for a population of lower-class wage earners. The most common offenses were burglary, bar fights, and a trickle of drug-related incidents. Prostitution was isolated along the waterfront and ignored except when some other problem called attention to it. Murders were extremely rare. Domestic abuse was hidden behind veils of family privacy; city social workers discreetly tended what surfaced in police calls and legal complaints. Divorces happened, but even in fishing and seagoing families from which the men strayed more easily, they were still uncommon. The city was losing its young people;

the economy was as shaky as it was everyplace else in Great Britain; the winters were long and boring.

Most of the people of Aberdeen thought that becoming the Scottish Klondike was the best thing that could ever happen to their city. In 1971, the chamber of commerce sent a delegation to the annual petroleum exposition in Houston, Texas. They went with no firm appointments with oil executives, checked into their hotel rooms, and started making blind calls. They asked only one question: "What can Aberdeen do for you?" The oilmen told them they wanted land on the waterfront, plenty of warehouse space at the airport, places to live, and a warm welcome. "Come and get it," said the businessmen from Aberdeen.

After Ekofisk, the Forties, and Brent, 25,000 new people and more than 15,000 new jobs hit Northeast Scotland like a tidal wave. In the early years of the boom, most of them were young Americans who arrived in a city full of men who couldn't dance and women who wanted to. Overnight, the predictable pace of family life that had included picnics, evenings at the greyhound track, and the movie matinees turned into a sexual free-for-all. Along the cobbled alleys leading down from Union Street to the waterfront, strip clubs, brothels, and bars transformed downtown into a boys' club. Aberdeen women were used to their men going away for fishing, whaling, the navy and merchant marine, but husbands working on oil rigs and in fabrication yards were different. Most of them came off their two- or three-week work shifts bottled up with reckless energy that didn't easily translate into domestic bliss.

A few years into the boom, a lot of people were wondering where all the money was. At Gilly's Bar in Houston, a hot request for the band was "Crew Change Night in Aberdeen." In Aberdeen, some of the locals were making killings as contractors servicing the rigs, buying big houses, and importing Lincoln Continentals and Ferraris. Three thousand American families moved into the city and lived on expense accounts. Single men working offshore in the higher-paid jobs as divers and drillers spent money like sailors on shore leave in Aberdeen for a few days, then took their paychecks back to Houston or London or wherever they were from. Most working-class

Scottish families, even those with men doing oil work, were struggling to make ends meet. The jobs the oilmen promised materialized, but the wages weren't much better than those of laborers or retail clerks. Only the fact that the men worked so much overtime made any difference at all. The price of food, gas, housing, and entertainment had more than doubled. Aberdeen became the most expensive city in Europe. If a man didn't have oil work, it was impossible for a household to survive. In the winter of 1973, a Scottish woman whose husband was working for BP complained about the transformation of the city at a cocktail party at the new Petroleum Club in Aberdeen. She had grown up on the banks of the Don, she said, and missed the old, slow days. A blond woman with spray-lacquered hair and a Texas accent touched her on the shoulder and cleared the air.

"Honey, if you want this town the way it was, you can't have the money. You just have to decide."

In the summer of 1974, the Aberdeen City Council took that decision out of the hands of the four hundred people living in Old Torry, a fishing settlement at the entrance to Aberdeen harbor. The three and a half acres on the south bank of the Dee had been permanently inhabited for more than a thousand years, first mentioned in an account of a Viking raid on the site in the twelfth century. The stone cottages and gear sheds were a Hollywood set of a Scottish fishing village, with a warren of narrow streets offset to the northeast against the prevailing weather and seas from the south, and a little lighthouse marking the entrance to its boat basin. A year earlier, while Aberdeen was still competing with Peterhead and Dundee to become Europe's oil capital, Shell Oil's advance man had issued his company's ultimatum. "We want a terminal for drilling mud, fuel storage, docks, and warehouses at Old Torry. If Aberdeen can't provide the facilities, we will look elsewhere." At a private meeting with Shell, the Aberdeen City Council granted Shell a thirty-one-year lease on the site.

"The Torry people were helpless against the oil companies," Mrs.

Elizabeth Finlayson told a *Press and Journal* reporter who was in Old Torry when people started moving out. "We'll never forget."

For a month, house after house emptied, their doors were padlocked, their windows shuttered with plywood. Finally, only Charlotte Simpson and her dog were left in the cottage that had been her home for twenty-one years. The Council had offered her a new house and £3,150 for moving expenses. She said she would stay until the bitter end. Nobody should be able to take away the house where she had spent her married life. Now, on a soggy gray morning, four policemen were there, backed by a gang of construction men. A knot of people who had already moved were back to see what was going to happen to their old friend. On the street, a big yellow and black backhoe grumbled, its claw bucket poised to take its first demolishing swipe at her old house. Charlotte stood in the doorway. There was no doubt of the outcome, no doubt that the police would never lay a hand on an old woman or that the backhoe wouldn't slam into the house until she left, no doubt that Charlotte would do what she finally did, which was start crying and walk over to disappear among her friends. Later, one of them would say to the reporter covering the demolition of Charlotte's house: "I guess we know what oil really costs."

Fourteen years after Charlotte Simpson lost her home to the oil boom, another woman living in an apartment not far from the bones of Old Torry would also learn what oil really costs. As the bell tower carillons of Aberdeen struck the single note of the quarter hour of 10:15 on July 6, 1988, Kate Graham had just finished catching up on her perpetually late expense account records. She was thirty-eight years old, grew up in Aberdeen, and had been one of the first people hired by Occidental Petroleum in 1975. Oxy vice president Elmer Daniel needed a secretary and Kate got the job. In his office, she had watched a steady parade of outlandish men whose Stetsons, silver belt buckles, and snakeskin boots echoed what she knew about America from the television series *Dallas*. Most of the people she worked with had come to Aberdeen straight from Libya. One of them was supposed to have been kicked out of the country for failing to be sure every Occidental employee showed up for a speech by Colonel Qaddafi. Graham had organized parties for Daniel, the first for a hundred and twenty people, the biggest for seven hundred when the first Occidental crude flowed from Piper Alpha to the terminal at Flotta on December 27, 1976. Daniel put her in charge of public relations a year later. Kate Graham loved her job, loved Oxy, loved Scotland. She was getting ready for bed when her phone rang. The person on the other end identified himself as a producer she knew from Grampian Television.

"There's been an explosion on Piper Alpha," he said. "By sheer luck, we have a camera crew out there on a chopper filming what we thought was going to be a routine safety patrol. The rig's on fire. Our crew is getting it on tape, but it'll be three or four hours before we get it. What have you heard?"

Graham said she'd call back. She dressed and was out the door in minutes to drive the few miles to Occidental headquarters north of the city.

On the way, she caught herself whispering, "No, don't let it be bad. Don't let it be bad."

Eight

PIPER ALPHA

While Kate Graham tore across Aberdeen in her car, the men on Piper Alpha were beginning to realize that what was happening on the rig might mean more than an early trip ashore. After the explosion just before ten o'clock, the floor of the passageway out-side the cinema was trembling so violently that flight logistics offi-cer Mike Jennings had to brace himself against the walls to walk. Suddenly, as though someone had cued a stage effect, the shaking eased slightly and the hallway began to fill with a black haze that made it nearly impossible to breathe. The fluorescent lights over-head flickered, went out, and were replaced by the weaker beams of the emergency lighting. Jennings bolted up the ladder. He detoured to his own cabin to grab his survival suit and glanced into the can-teen at a crowd of about forty men looking confused but not pan-icked. A minute later, he was at the door to the radio room on the top deck of the accommodation module to the south of the helideck. The wind was blowing thick dark smoke up the side of the rig and across the landing pad. Unless something changed right away, there was no chance that a helicopter could land on Piper Alpha. The lifeboats and *Tharos* were the only hope for evacuation other than jumping into the North Sea.

In the radio room, offshore installation manager Colin Seaton, dressed in an orange survival suit, stood behind radio operator David Kinrade. Seaton had shouldered his way through knots of puzzled men from his office four decks below. When he emerged onto an exterior stairway at the top of the accommodation stack, Seaton saw dense smoke and flames pouring from the production deck, cutting off the north and west faces of the rig where the life-boats hung on their davits. Two hundred and twenty-five men were waiting for his orders. Seaton grabbed the loudspeaker mike, clicked the button, and said "Attention all hands." The monitor speaker was silent. Seaton tried it again. Nothing. He told Kinrade to send a Mayday. The radio was drawing power from emergency batteries that had come online automatically in the minutes since the explosion. Kinrade, infected by the unmistakable overtones of panic in the OIM, tuned to the emergency distress frequency and stuttered out Piper Alpha's plea for help.

"Mayday. Mayday. We require any assistance available, any assistance available. We've had an explosion and er . . . a very bad explosion and fire er . . . the radio room is badly damaged."

Jennings looked into the radio room and saw one wall tilted inward. Part of the ceiling dangled from wire hangers exposing the innards of the duct system. "Don't stay here," Seaton yelled over his shoulder at Jennings. There was a smaller standby radio room on the west side of the platform, but Jennings had already seen the dense smoke and flames sweeping across the helideck, which he would have to cross to get there. It would be suicide to try. With the radio rooms and the helipad out of commission, Jennings was on his own. He headed for the galley one deck below. Trotting down the interior ladders with his survival suit tucked under his arm, he felt heat rising from the metal decks through his heavy rig boots. It seemed impossible that any of the hundred and fifty men who were off duty in their cabins were still asleep or zoned out into their Walkmen or TVs, but Jennings instinctively banged on the walls of the corridor as he descended.

In one of the cabins, Ian Gillanders fought his way out of the shower with one arm holding up a panel of the fiberglass wall that had collapsed on his head. He hadn't lost consciousness, but he was groggy. At fifty, Gillanders was an old man for life offshore. A plumber by trade from a village near Inverness, he had been on the rigs for five years since jobs in the fabrication yards in north-ern Scotland dried up. He and his wife, Ann, owned a gift shop called Choices and were saving money for some kind of business big enough to support them and their two college-age children. At

Ardersier, Gillanders had helped build Piper Alpha. By coincidence, he found himself aboard the big rig as a pipefitter fifteen years later wondering how such a sorry piece of junk had survived that long. When his roommates Charlie McLaughlin and Bob Ballantyne burst into the cabin, he was dazed, naked and shivering. The foul stink of burning oil, paint, and scorched metal followed them into the cabin. McLaughlin threw him a towel. Ballantyne had been in the laundry room when the explosion happened. He slung a bag of clothes onto his lower bunk, from which Gillanders grabbed a set of coveralls and put them on.

"There are men in survival suits and breathing gear all over the place," Ballantyne said. "Get your passport, money if you have it. We're getting off the rig. We could end up in Bergen or who knows where." McLaughlin joked that they'd need money for drinks no matter where the choppers put them ashore. Ballantyne came back with, "Fucking Oxy will probably let us rot."

Ballantyne was an electrician from Glasgow, a passionate trade unionist who had been fired from more jobs offshore than he could count because he couldn't contain his contempt for the oil companies' shabby treatment of workingmen. He was forty-five, had slowed down a bit in his quest for a fair universe and the socialist dream, and had held his job with a contractor on Piper Alpha for a year and a half. He was the resident intellectual with a salty beard and longish hair who brought a bag of textbooks offshore to work on a degree in philosophy from the Scottish Open University. There were no jobs ashore during the late eighties and riding out the recession on an oil rig gave him plenty of time to read. While he toned down his anticorporate, anti-Thatcher diatribes, Ballantyne could not resist railing about the deplorable condition of the rigs on which the lives of oil workers depended. He thought Piper Alpha was no better or worse than most of them, but suspected that all of them were hydrocarbon time bombs. He knew for sure that to Occidental Petroleum, he was no more valuable than an interchangeable part on a pump.

When Mike Jennings took off for the radio room, Bill Barron and the rest of the men from the cinema headed for the galley one deck up where they expected to be told what to do. They walked in an orderly quickstep, all of them used to easing around each other in narrow passageways. Their mingled voices were barely audible above what sounded like a huge Bunsen burner, but the tone was one of gathering fear as wisps of smoke seeped into the corridor from overhead and through the air ducts. Should we go down to the lifeboats? Up to the galley and the helideck? Somebody opened a door to one of the exterior staircases at the north end of the accommodation module and they saw black smoke threaded with whiskers of flame rising from the production deck below. It looked to Barron like a diesel oil fire. If the explosion and fire were coming from down there, there was no way they were going to get to their lifeboats or whatever was left of them. Any doubts they had about going up to the canteen and the helideck vanished.

The top of the stairway to the accommodation module opened into a reception area from which an L-shaped corridor led into the canteen itself. Barron and the others from the cinema got as far as the first turn of the L and saw what looked like fifty men milling around inside. Nobody was giving orders, but everyone seemed calm. Barron turned around and started working his way against the line of men trying to get into the big room. He knew he was supposed to muster at his lifeboat if he could and in the canteen if he couldn't. Barron was wearing slippers. He was going to need something better on his feet. For two minutes, he elbowed his way past a steady stream of men, some of them soot-black, some with cuts and scratches, some scorched red on their hands and faces. Barron darted into his cabin, grabbed his passport, boots, and life vest, turned around and ran headlong into Barry Goodwin. Goodwin was Piper Alpha's rigging boss, a North Sea veteran who did his time offshore stoically in much the same way as Barron. Neither man wasted words. They had shared an office on A Deck for two years.

Barron and Goodwin agreed to stick together. Up or down was still the question. Barron told him what he had seen in the canteen and about the flames out the door after he left the cinema. It looked like the fire on the production deck was between them and the lifeboats. Every passageway and compartment in the accommodation module was getting smokier by the minute, but they decided their best bet was to try the canteen once more. If the OIM evacuated the rig by chopper or directly to *Tharos* over a gangway, he would come to the canteen to give the order. Barron and Goodwin worked their way back, pressing more than once against the wall of the corridor to make way for the injured. If they had any doubts that their lives were in danger, they were banished by two dazed men carrying a third, limp and covered with blood, who passed them on the way to the sick bay.

The crowd in the canteen had grown to seventy-five or eighty. It looked to Barron like a bunch of men waiting for a meal except for the wisps of smoke against the yellowish light through the windows on the north and west sides of the room. The ceiling panel bulbs were dark, replaced by a dim glow from strips of emergency lights on the floor. The fish tank lights were still on, so some power was getting through. Barron surveyed the scene: most of the men stood or sat at the tables anchored to the floor, their arms folded over their chests, their eyes darting to any movement expecting someone in authority to tell them what to do next. A few who had come from their workstations were in coveralls, a few had survival suits still in their bags, most were in the oilmen's lounging pajamas of sweat pants and shirts. Barron couldn't remember ever having been in the canteen when the murmur of conversation was not punctuated by laughter but nobody was joking. He heard bursts of expletives, the "fuck all" of an Aberdonian, the drawn out "Jeeesuuus Christ" of an American, the hard edges of a British "bloody hell." He smelled the same kind of smoke that had infiltrated the corridors in the accommodation module, a gassy muck with an ozone bite to it that was definitely getting worse. A steady stream of men filed into the room, most leaning into the ears of those already there to ask what was happening. Over the other voices, somebody said he'd come from D Module and there was a pool of diesel fuel on fire near the lifeboats. Another man said the fire was coming up the side of the rig and spilling over onto the helideck. How the fuck are we going to evacuate by chopper? Does anybody know what's going on? Twenty minutes after the explosion, more than a hundred men were in the galley. The emergency lights flickered and went out leaving only the gurgling glow from the two fish tanks. The room was rife with misgivings, but the men stayed put because they were trained to stay put. Most of them had spent their lives in jobs that forced them to bend to authority, so they were deeply conditioned to do what their superiors told them to do.

Twelve miles from Piper Alpha, Tartan's manager John Leeming heard the Maydays and saw an orange glow in the sky over the rig. He told his radioman to stay tuned to the emergency frequency and ordered his production crew to watch the pressure in the eighteen-inch pipeline through which Tartan was pumping gas to Piper Alpha. Unless he heard otherwise from Texaco onshore, he wasn't shutting down his rig or the gas line. Leeming knew that keeping pressure in the line could feed a fire on Piper Alpha, but he was betting that the explosion was just a gas storage tank blowing like it had in 1984 when Piper had been evacuated. The crew should be able to handle it without shutting down the network of pipelines through which millions of Texaco and Occidental dollars a day were flowing to shore. A crash shutdown would mean irreparable damage to countless valves, pumps, and wellheads that took weeks to bring back online. He'd wait for the shutdown order from shore. If it came, he'd take his rig off-line slowly, with the least amount of damage to his production.

Twenty-two miles away on Occidental's Claymore platform, manager S. B. Sandlin knew even less about what was happening on Piper Alpha than Leeming on Tartan. He couldn't see the flames. After his radioman picked up the first Mayday, he told him to raise Occidental headquarters in Aberdeen for instructions. Sandlin left the radio room on the top deck of the accommodation module and clattered down five decks to the main control room to find out what was happening with his own wells and pipelines. He knew there was no gas flowing from Piper Alpha because of the maintenance shutdown, but gas from Tartan and Claymore went through Piper Alpha to connect with the MCP-01 pumping platform and on to shore. In the control room, Sandlin scanned the instruments monitoring the flow to and from his rig and saw nothing wrong. Whatever was happening on Piper Alpha hadn't affected the production flow. No shutdown. Sandlin had been aboard Claymore when Piper Alpha blew in 1984. He didn't shut down then and it was a good decision. One of the production operators, James Davidson, told Sandlin he was dead wrong. Davidson turned from the panel, glared at Sandlin, and told him that until they knew more, the right decision was definitely to shut down Claymore, depressurize the pipelines, and clear them with air. The men, Davidson said. The men. Enough gas was flowing through the pipelines to launch Piper Alpha and all its men to the moon if it blew. No shutdown until we hear from Aberdeen, Sandlin said.

On a catwalk outside Claymore's control room, rigger Keith Ellis watched a false dawn glimmering to the northeast across the blackening surface of the summer-calm sea. Ellis looked at his watch. Ten-twenty-one. His brother David was a cook on Piper Alpha. A minute later, what had been a faint orange glow on the horizon blossomed gracefully into a bright yellow hump like one of those A-bomb test films Ellis had seen in school.

Nine

THE DIVERS

Underwater, Gareth Parry-Davies had seen the first explosion as a white flash in the periphery of his vision. The light was gone in the same instant it appeared, replaced by a bass-toned thump like a punch from a huge soft rubber fist. The chatter of the sandblaster he was holding stopped. His training commanded him to stay calm and assess what was happening before he made a move. Ten seconds after the thud, the light came back, brighter now with an orange cast to it that blossomed in the sea all around him. Okay, he thought. Hose rupture. Maybe that was the noise. What the hell was the light? Ten more seconds.

"Drop everything. Go to the bell. Do it," John Barr said, his voice modulated like that of a military squad leader under fire.

The bell was unpressurized and open to the water. Parry-Davies swam the fifteen feet to it in five seconds, worried all the time that his umbilical might snag.

"Watch the hose," he barked into his helmet mike.

"Got it. Got it," Barr came back. "We got it up here."

The flash and thud that stunned Parry-Davies underwater had knocked Barr off his chair. He had picked himself up and saw that the floor around him was littered with manuals and papers that had fallen from shelves and filing cabinets. The overhead sprinklers spewed water for a few seconds, then stopped. The monitors were dark. The voice line was still alive. He checked the airflow gauge on the analog panel. Good. If Parry-Davies could breathe he had a chance. Barr stumbled to the door. Two divers were still there, tending the umbilical cord and diving bell winches as Parry-Davies ascended. A third diver, Keith Cunningham, burst down the ladder to the dive platform wearing an emergency breathing apparatus. Just that evening, Cunningham had been talking in the Wendy Hut about being aboard Piper Alpha for the explosion and evacuation in '84. He had joked that the tatty old rig was overdue for another catastrophe. Cunningham yelled something that was muffled by his face mask and the roar of the flare booms on the corners of the rig. He frantically pointed up. The air on the dive platform was clear, but flames flickered through the ceiling around an elbow joint in the thirty-inch main pipeline that ran horizontally under the plating of the deck above.

Barr heard a phone ringing behind him in Dive Control. He pivoted through the door to snatch it off the desk.

"Is anybody still in the water?" Stan McCleod barked on the other end.

Barr told him that Parry-Davies was in the bell and on the way up. McCleod said that there had been an explosion powerful enough to spring the door on one of the decompression chambers. The lights were off in the other chamber but it looked like it would still work. Use that one for Parry-Davies. He didn't know how bad it was, but there was smoke and fire on Sixty-eight. Muster at lifeboat stations. McCleod hung up.

Seconds later, the diving bell materialized in the eerily serene water beneath Piper Alpha. With the efficiency that comes from thousands of repetitions, the divers eased the bell to the platform. Parry-Davies emerged, dripping and confused, looking from man to man for some reassurance that whatever was happening was some kind of minor glitch. Barr grabbed him by the arm and hustled him up the stairway to the deco chamber.

Parry-Davies had made an emergency ascent. He could get the bends unless he depressurized more slowly in the chamber. Barr led him up the ladder. Both men were stunned to see the heavy steel hatch of one of the chambers hanging like the broken neck of a bird. Dark smoke blowing across Sixty-eight obscured the dive offices only a few feet away. Barr shoved Parry-Davies in the direction of the undamaged chamber. Parry-Davies thought, Do I want to be climbing into a deco chamber with a fire burning across the deck?

Not sure enough of himself to disobey Barr, Parry-Davies climbed into the chamber, flipped open the bunk, and sat down.

"What the fuck?" he said as Barr slammed the hatch and dogged it down. The lights inside the chamber were out. Parry-Davies glanced at the chronometer on his wrist. 10:06. Only five minutes had passed since he felt the sea convulse and saw the water brighten around him. He felt the pressure in the chamber build to match that of the two atmospheres in which he had been working underwater. Barr stared at him through the thick round porthole in the door, looking bewildered and frightened. A long minute passed before the worn, jowly face of Stan McCleod replaced Barr's in the porthole. Parry-Davies heard the farting of the vents releasing pressure and the door swung open.

McCleod and Barr stood there, shockingly pale with smoke whirling around them and sheets of what looked like liquid fire moving across the floor. McCleod fumbled with a breathing mask and finally got it on.

"You're probably good," Barr said to Parry-Davies as he helped him from the chamber. "Stay in your suit. Let's get the hell out of here."

The other divers materialized in the smoke from the dive platform below, with about six men waiting on the ladder. Barry Barber, the Occidental dive rep, shouted their names from the door of the office and ticked them off a list on a clipboard when a man said "Here," or "Yo." Near the edge of the deck, flames erupted around a pile of fifty-five-gallon drums of rig wash, a solvent used for cleaning the perpetually oily surfaces. Next to them was a clutch of oxygen bottles that would turn into fragmentation bombs if they ignited.

Immediately after the explosion, when McCleod ordered him to fuck off to his lifeboat, Ed Punchard had taken off on the run. Sixty-eight was obviously on fire, so he dropped down to the cellar deck twenty feet below and crossed the northwest corner where a ladder would take him around it and up to the eighty-five-foot level. Then it would be only another twenty feet to the boats. As he ran, he glanced over the side at the *Lowland Cavalier,* which was stern-to at the base of the rig. Its crew had been tending the remotely operated video camera that was working on the Chanter riser. Now, Punchard saw them cutting the cables to the ROV and throwing them over the side. Smoke roared from *Lowland Cavalier*'s twin stacks as the boat pulled away.

"Fucking hell," Punchard thought, then realized he had spoken aloud. "This must be bad. That ROV was worth ten million bucks."

When Punchard reached the bottom of the ladder on the northwest corner, three men in Occidental coveralls clanked down helping a fourth whose arm hung in front of him like it was numb.

"Forget it," one of them said. "Don't bother trying to get up there. There's no way up. It's all blocked with smoke and fire."

Punchard thought the man had to be exaggerating. He turned and trotted back in the direction of the dive complex, confident that he'd find a way up to the lifeboats on the other side of it. He turned the corner off the catwalk at the side of the dive offices and saw fire and smoke in the center of the platform to the east. It didn't look too bad. The flames seemed to be coming from a small oil fire near one of the injection pumps, but it wasn't burning hot enough to be gas. Any fire on an oil rig was bad news, but what he saw gave him hope that they might be able to put it out. On the other side of the office, he saw the Oxy dive rep Barber, McCleod, and a tight cluster of maybe ten other men. A broken electrical cable was flopping on the deck like a runaway garden hose, sending out blue arcs on every bounce. Beyond it, the southern end of the deck was obscured by thick black smoke. Punchard couldn't see where it was coming from.

As the Occidental dive boss, Barber was in charge, standing there with his clipboard, his eyes flashing from the arcing cable to the flames in the center of the rig.

"I've phoned the control room," Barber said to Punchard. "The lines are dead. So is the radio. Everything's broken down. I don't know a thing." By the time he finished talking, Punchard recognized panic in Barber's tightly controlled voice.

"We can't go south," Punchard said. "The oxygen bottles are over there, and we can see the flames from here. If that blows it'll bring down a whole block of flats on its own."

"Okay," Barber said, glancing at McCleod, then at Punchard as though for approval. "Let's go north."

"No way," Punchard said. "I tried it once and the northwest stairwell was blocked. You want me to try again?"

"Do it," Barber said. "If you're not back in a couple of minutes I'll know it's okay."

Punchard turned to another diver, Andy Carrol, who had just arrived from below. "You with me?" Carrol nodded and they ran back toward the northwest corner.

Punchard was acutely aware of the wind direction. The fire he had seen around the injection pump couldn't be the only thing burning because there was dense smoke blowing in from the southwest that completely obscured the center of the deck. The northwest corner should be upwind. Staying upwind in a fire on an oil rig was critical because there was a good chance that the wind carried deadly gas as well as smoke. Burning hydrogen sulfide, an evil-smelling swamp gas that rose from the depths of the earth in crude oil, could kill you in seconds.

Punchard and Carrol reached the bottom of the northwest staircase where several men were tending to the injured man who had been carried down a few minutes before on Punchard's first reconnaissance. Nobody seemed panicked.

"It can't be all that serious," one of them said. "They still haven't set off the fire alarms."

"Perhaps they can't," another man said.

"Don't be bloody daft."

Punchard had no sense of imminent danger. He assumed that he and everybody else would be onshore in a few hours having a couple of pints in a pub.

"If we're going to get out of here," Carrol said, snapping Punchard from his reverie, "we've got to get up those bloody stairs."

"It's blocked up there, mate," one of the other men said. "You might get trapped if you go up."

"We'll bloody well be trapped if we stay here," Carrol said. "The fucking lifeboats and the helideck are up there."

Punchard slapped Carrol on the shoulder and took off up the stairs. It would only take him a minute or two to find out if the way was clear or not, another minute to get back to Barber and lead him and the other divers to safety. With Carrol on his heels, Punchard bolted up the stairs, feeling heat in the steel handrails and sensing increasing warmth in the air with every step he took. On the landing on the eighty-five-foot level, a gust of dense black smoke washed over them, making their eyes burn. They could feel the heat but couldn't see the fire. Ten steps in on Eighty-five toward the stairway that would lead up to the 107-foot level, Punchard caught a glimpse of the lifeboats that quickly disappeared in a whirlpool of flame and smoke billowing down from above. There was no way they were going to reach them.

Punchard and Carrol ran back down to the northwest corner of Eighty-five near the head of the stairs where fifteen or so men were standing around like they were waiting for a bus.

"What the hell are we doing standing here?" one of them shouted.

"Waiting for some bugger to tell us what to do," somebody else said, with a note of resignation.

"And who's that going to be?"

"The control room, who do you think?"

"No fucking way. I was there," another man said. Punchard recognized one of the production men, Geoff Bollands. "There's wires hanging down everywhere. Even the bloody bulkheads have buckled in. The explosion blew me straight across the fucking room on my chair."

For the first time, it occurred to Punchard that the only way off Piper Alpha might be to jump. It was the stuff of horror stories passed around the rigs, stories of men hitting the water wrong from just thirty feet up and drowning before they regained consciousness. Grim accounts of men dropping from a hundred feet and hitting so hard that the water rushed up their assholes with enough force to explode their insides; the assurances of safety trainers that the odds for surviving a jump from above a hundred feet were a thousand to one. Punchard leaned over the rail. The sea eighty-five feet below was a dark, undulating mat that looked as hard as a sheet of steel. The wind shifted. The air on the northwest corner that had been clear was now thickening with smoke and carrying burning embers from the middle of the rig. Worse, Punchard heard the shrill, unmis-

takable howl of escaping gas from somewhere inside the conflagration. If I don't move, I'll die, he thought. He and the men who had
been waiting for someone to tell them what to do came to the same
conclusion at the same time and started down to Sixty-eight.

At the foot of the stairs, Punchard ran into Barber, who was at
the head of an orderly column of a dozen divers. "What's going on
up there, Ed?"

"God only knows, but there's no way up. It's blazing up there,"
Punchard said.

Somebody said, "There's a box of life jackets here, chaps. Let's
get them on," and the men began passing them down the line.

The wind shifted again, this time driven by some hot force other
than itself that was growing in the center of the rig. The refuge on
the northwest corner of Sixty-eight was blanketed by foul-smelling
smoke that would kill them even more surely than fire if they didn't
get moving. They knew there were going to be no orders from
anyone in authority. It was starkly clear that it was every man for
himself.

Punchard went for a ladder that led ten feet further down to a
small platform for one of the red navigation beacons that warned
ships away from the rig. As he went over, he heard a man shout,
"That's a dead end, Ed. It don't go nowhere."

"I don't care," Punchard yelled back. "I just want to get a better
look at what's happening."

Because he was under the sixty-eight-foot deck, he could see that
the whole dive complex was ablaze. The heat hit him in the face
like he had opened an oven door. Fire was now consuming the dive
offices, decompression chambers, and Dive Control. Flaming debris
the size of automobiles was falling from the upper decks. A man
passed down a knotted rope and shouted, "There's only one way off
this fucker." Punchard grabbed the rope, swung away from the navigation platform, and shinnied down to the lattice of catwalks and
guardrails known as the Spider Deck. Before he let go of the rope,
he looked up and saw another man already descending. Since the
explosion in the dive office, Punchard had been running on automatic pilot, pure reflex in the face of danger. Now, the possibility of
death made him desperate to see his daughter, Suzie. Like a jolt of

electricity coursing through him came the thought about his phone conversation with Vicky that afternoon. The tension of offshore life was wearing on them. They both hated telephone calls. Something had to give.

"I've got the feeling that something big is going to happen," Ed had told Vicky before they hung up. "Something that's really going to change everything."

Ten

ABERDEEN

Twenty minutes after Kate Graham took her first call from the Grampian TV producer just after 10:00 p.m., television newsrooms all over Britain were chasing the Piper Alpha story. A fire on the biggest oil rig in the world was a disaster on a grand scale.

Over the years, Kenny and Linda Clarke's nightly routine had matured into the comforts of a cup of tea and the late news before they went to bed. That night, Linda was in the living room with the TV, Kenny was in the kitchen with the tea. Both of them had been born in Aberdeen, felt comfortable tossing the lilting phrases of old Doric around the house, and from the beginning suspected that no good would come of the flood of Americans and their money. Kenny was an out of work engineer in the depression of the seventies. Despite his misgivings he had no choice but to take a job in the oil rig fabrication yard at Arderseir. He just did what he had to do. Kenny was one of those Scotsmen with a stoic exterior that could take him to war on a moment's notice and a heart so soft he had trouble getting through a couple of drinks and a chorus of "Loch Lomond" without puddling up.

"Piper Alpha's on the telly again," Linda said, her voice almost a whisper, just loud enough to carry the ten feet into the kitchen. She was watching the end of the Independent Television News program, a matter-of-fact recitation of national and local events that was a staple of many homes in Northeast Scotland. "He says it's on fire. No pictures."

Kenny turned off the kettle. "I know men on that rig," he said, propping himself in the doorway to the living room. "It's a real piece of shit." The announcer said that ITV would broadcast further bulletins as they came in through the night.

Like everyone whose lives were entangled with North Sea oil, the Clarkes had absorbed a lot of bad news from offshore. They had heard about dead men, injured men, one or two at a time, many of whom they knew or knew someone who knew them. The Clarkes were especially tuned to Piper Alpha because Kenny had gone from Arderseir to the hookup crew when Oxy's big rig went to work. He came home from the hookup job with a bitterness in him about Occidental and the other companies. Kenny railed that the oil business didn't give a damn about the men like him who were out there risking their lives while they made fortunes for tycoons and stockholders. Two years later, he was laid off when oil prices collapsed, one of the first men to go because he had become a grumbler whose every day in the oil business was like a grim forced march. For fifteen years, he worked offshore and onshore. Three times, he was not required back by oil field contractors, not once with more than his last paycheck in his pocket.

"Anybody who thinks those bastards did us a favor by coming here to take the oil is making a big fucking mistake," he said, glaring at the television. "Oil killed Scotland and we're never going to get it back." Linda looked over her shoulder at her husband and saw tears in his eyes.

At the Royal Infirmary on the western edge of Aberdeen, Dr. Graham Page watched the end of the same ITV nightly news on a portable television. He was on duty as the chief of the emergency room, wondering why he hadn't heard from the police or the coast guard before getting the news of a possible disaster on TV. Page tried to call both and got the irritating bleats of busy signals. He slumped in his chair and took a minute to make his decision. The announcer had said Piper Alpha. A big platform, more than two hundred men, he reckoned. He thought it was impossible that he would get that many, but he had to prepare for that many beds. Surgeries. A burn ward. Blood. Doctors and nurses. It would take hours to get everything moving. Page decided he couldn't wait. He pulled a three-ring binder from a bookshelf over his desk and started ticking through his instructions for the infirmary's major disaster plan.

He tried the police station again. Still busy. Coast guard. The same. Then he began dialing the numbers on his plan. Doctors. Nurses. Social workers. Porters. Radiology. Records. Nobody would be glad to hear from him.

Between his second and third calls, his own phone rang under his finger as he was depressing the disconnect button. It was somebody from Grampian Television who asked if Graham knew what was happening on Piper Alpha. Only what I saw on ITV, he said. He had no idea how bad it was. He was preparing for the worst. Page hung up and dialed a number from further down on his list, Archie Robb, the deputy director of social services for Northeast Scotland. In practice disasters, Robb had directed his social workers in the delicate business of helping people in crisis find food and shelter, and tending the more difficult trauma of grief. The plan also called for Robb to help the police manage inquiries about survivors, victims, and their families.

Archie Robb was born into fishing families on both his father's and mother's sides. His family had been running trawlers out of Peterhead for generations. Like most fishermen, the Robbs believed that the best thing that could happen to their sons was to find an easier way than fighting the North Sea to make a living. Archie went to university in Aberdeen and did his best to realize his parents' intentions by working in a bank. Ten years later, Robb was so bored and disillusioned with the pragmatism of money that he invented a new life for himself. In 1968, just as the first hints of the North Sea boom rolled over coastal Scotland, Robb quit the bank and went back to school to become a social worker. He was a soft-spoken man with a soothing demeanor that was perfectly suited not only for compassionate fieldwork but also for the steady routines of government work.

Robb had joined a well-entrenched bureaucracy that oversaw child protection, adoptions, foster care, parole, mental health, home care, and elder services for a population of 350,000 centered in Aberdeen and radiating around the Highlands. Before the oil, during his first ten years on the job, most of the trouble he encountered in families rose from Scotland's celebrated culture of alcohol and the stresses of unemployment during the economic collapse.

The oil brought more of the same, but with a heavier load from single-parent households and troubled children after the epidemic of divorce set in. Something about oil work dismantled families with such regularity it was as if dismal outcomes were intentional. Archie Robb and his family had been immune to it all. He was asleep in bed with his wife, Norma, when Graham Page called to tell him to come to the hospital.

Like a grim rumor, the news of a fire on Piper Alpha spread around Northeast Scotland from person to person. Jane Franchi, the British Broadcasting correspondent in Aberdeen, was in her office on the phone with the coast guard duty officer trying to find out if what she had heard from a source at Grampian TV might be another of the endless false alarms she dealt with. Just that week, there had already been three reports of trouble offshore that amounted to nothing. No, the officer told her. This looked big. There definitely had been an explosion on Piper Alpha. Two ships sent out Maydays that a rig was on fire. Franchi called the airport. It usually closed at 9:30 on summer nights. She wanted to know if it had been reopened to land evacuation choppers. The airport was still closed. She called the coast guard again. This time, the duty officer's voice had a tone of studied restraint, like he had been practicing all his life to deliver bad news.

"Piper Alpha is burning from the top of the derrick to sea level."

The BBC evening news was over. Franchi convinced the on-air producer of the late night newsmagazine to shoehorn her one-minute phone report on Piper Alpha into the end of the show. There are more than twenty-five thousand men working offshore, she told him. Most of their wives and girlfriends have no idea where they are working. They have to know what's happening.

The wives and girlfriends whose men worked offshore had grown accustomed to not knowing what their husbands and lovers were doing. Sometimes, they weren't even sure which rig he was on, or even if he had left Aberdeen. The oil boom's dramatic transformation of the once milder culture of Scotland was a constant source of human interest features.

"The offshore life allowed my husband to deceive himself," one of them said on a talk show. "I'd say to him, 'You know you drink too much,' and he would answer, 'No, I don't. I can go two weeks without drinking.' Of course, if you haven't got any alcohol you can get through two weeks, but it doesn't mean you are any less desperate for it. I know he used to suffer when he was offshore and couldn't drink.

"For us, the North Sea was either fast or feast. When my husband was working he earned £120 a week. Our rent was only £7. We were able to go out and buy whatever we liked for the house. But another time, he was out of work for eighteen months. One day, I lost a £1 note in the street. I'll never forget walking up and down in tears trying to find it, thinking that we had no money to feed our two children.

"For two weeks, I was a single parent, able to make decisions and social contacts outside my relationship. Then my husband came home. He was usually very tired. And he wanted alcohol, which was banned offshore. For the first five days he simply disrupted our lifestyle. After that, things would calm down and he'd want a family life, by which time my children and I were usually too angry to participate. In the end, we used to look forward to him going away again.

"The shifts varied, but at one point my husband was away for seven weeks. I rang up the company and asked when they were sending him back. They said, 'Oh, he was onshore two weeks ago.' That's how I discovered my husband was having an affair. I suspect that not many marriages have survived from those days."

Not many of the Piper Alpha women heard the news that night. In Cornwall, far to the south of Aberdeen, Vicky Punchard rested easy with her daughter, Suzie, on the bed next to her. Ed was coming home the next day. They had talking to do that couldn't be done on the phone. He had been gone five weeks, and it felt like a lifetime. Trish Barron, in Aberdeen, rarely stayed up past the beginning of the late news. By seven the next morning, she had to be up and out to the laundry for ten hours of pressing shirts. In Glasgow,

Mary Reid, whose husband, Mark, was a driller on Piper Alpha, had been out with the girls and gotten home when there was no reason to turn on the telly. Kay Harney, in Portlethan, went to bed before the news, thinking about her last conversation with Eddie and all the talk about getting married. She loved him, but marrying a man working offshore was a long shot. She was getting too old to fail at it again. In Nairn, just outside of Inverness, Ann Gillanders didn't see the ITV news. Her daughter, Yvonne, did. Yvonne couldn't remember what rig her father, Ian, was on, but she didn't wake her mother to ask her. Morning would be soon enough.

Eleven

THE CANTEEN

During the twenty minutes after the first explosion, seventy or eighty men had gathered in Piper Alpha's canteen. The emergency lighting flickered on for a couple of minutes at the beginning, but since then only the hint of twilight through the windows and the jittery beams of flashlights gave the room dimension. The canteen was the largest enclosed compartment in the accommodation module, usually a place apart from the tedium of twelve-hour workdays, the one place with which every man was familiar. Because of its size and proximity to the helicopter pad fifteen feet above, it was the only sensible place other than the lifeboats to gather the rig's crew in an emergency. Now, the canteen was deteriorating into dark, smoky chaos. A few men tried to calm those who were succumbing to panic, but the mustering point for evacuation from Piper Alpha was becoming mobbed. Most men retreated into the solitude of survival, setting themselves apart at precisely the time when they needed each other the most.

In the dim, sooty light, the refuge of the galley had been transformed into a cramped encampment of bewildered men. About half of them were wearing life vests or survival suits. Some sat at tables, some leaned against a wall. A few hunkered on their haunches nearer the floor to get out of the smoke. In the minutes since the explosion, the fire had given way to dark black smoke. An ominous whooshing sound flowed with the smoke into the canteen through every door and vent. Much of the murmuring conversation in the galley was about the smoke. Some of the men argued that dark smoke and no flame probably meant that any fires started by an explosion were out. Others said that unless somebody got them out of there soon, they were going to suffocate, fire or no fire. Most said nothing.

A shout broke the din. Flashlight beams sliced into the haze to illuminate a man clambering onto one of the tables in the center of the canteen. Colin Seaton, the OIM, wearing his survival suit. He stood up and waved his hard hat in front of his face against the smoke. A man sitting just below him yelled, "Get us the fuck out of here." Seaton growled, "Shut up and stay calm. I've got four men out there in breathing gear looking for a way to the boats. Stay calm." His voice carried no conviction, none of the reassurance of command. "Ah, blow it out your ass," another man shouted. Seaton was not a popular OIM. He was English, which didn't help at a time when the battle cry "Scottish oil" had been resurrected by the always lurking Scottish separatist movement.

"Stay calm. I've sent Maydays," Seaton gasped, belying his authority in the tone of his words. The man was obviously coming apart. "The choppers are on the . . ." The OIM's voice faded into the clamor of heckling and fear. After a long minute during which his words had no calming effect on the men below him, the smoke overcame Seaton. He lurched off the table, barked into his handheld radio, heard static when he put it to his ear, and stumbled toward the door to reception.

In the time Seaton had been on the table, the floor of the canteen got noticeably hotter. The increasingly claustrophobic terror of being trapped took over the room. The smoke made it impossible to see. The men lying down on the floor got to their knees for a few seconds of relief from the heat, then dropped down again when they couldn't breathe in the smoke. The dim-lit haze took on a reddish tint as flame flashed in the windows on the north wall. Somebody shouted from the reception area that the lifeboats were on fire. No one had heard any choppers clatter onto the landing pad above them. The men nearest to the fish tanks reached into them for water to splash on their heads. When the water was gone, the fish flapped on the gravel for a few seconds and were still.

A hundred feet below the canteen, the fire that had begun in the condensate injection pump and spread to the diesel fuel tanks on the production deck enveloped most of the sixty-eight-foot level. Because the water intakes were off and switched to manual, the fire-fighting nozzles plumbed into the ceiling were dry. Soon after ignition, the fire had compromised joints and valves in the thirty-inch main oil pipeline, releasing crude oil into the conflagration. Like a burning lake three hundred feet square, the fire flowed around the top of the sixteen-inch gas pipeline connecting Piper Alpha to the Tartan platform eleven miles away. The steel walls of the pipe were thick enough to contain the gas under pressure of 1,800 pounds per square inch. The temperature of the steel rose to 1,300 degrees Fahrenheit in twenty minutes, at which point it lost the strength to contain the immense pressure. The explosion vaporized the blow-out preventer at the top of the pipeline in the center of Sixty-eight, releasing a blue-orange column of fire through the center of the rig and seven hundred feet into the night. The Tartan pipeline contained more than a million and a half cubic feet of gas. It burst upward and ignited in a microsecond, after which the gas continued to flow and feed the fire.

On Tartan, manager John Leeming had decided not to shut down his rig when the first fire appeared on the horizon. He was not going to order a shutdown that could cost his company millions of dollars without more information. At the burning top of the Tartan pipeline on Piper Alpha, the steel of the rig melted as though heated by a giant Bunsen burner. Above it, in the canteen, the temperature rose fifty degrees in an instant.

Mark Reid, a driller foreman, knew he was going to die. He didn't want to die among strangers. The thought formed in his mind in an instant. He wanted to be holding the hand of a friend. Around him, the bullet shots of cracking window glass punctuated the din of shouts and murmurs, a staccato beat that ticked off each worsening moment. Some men were crying.

"Is anybody here from Bawden Drilling?" Reid stumbled over to the condiment counter, grabbed a Styrofoam cup, dipped it into the open top of one of the juice dispensers, and poured sticky black currant punch over his head to cool himself off. Fear seized him with such force that he lost control, lurching from man to man around the room looking for someone he knew. Everyone was down on the floor. Some of the men were not moving. Those who could fended off Reid's snatching hands and screamed at him in vain to shut up.

Reid had been aboard Piper Alpha for less than twenty-four hours, arriving that morning on the shift-change chopper from Aberdeen. He was in his late twenties, a slim, athletic man from Glasgow who sported a gold earring and short, tough-guy haircut. His pretty wife, Mary, was at home with their thirteen-month-old son, Marc. Drillers were the princes of oil rigs, the men who actually found and lifted up the oil from deep in the earth. Reid liked being one of them. What drillers did was almost alchemy, miles of delicately threaded pipe, a hardened-steel bit churning through rock and dirt, deep reservoirs of oil under high pressure. They treated each other like members of a secret society.

"Is anyone here from Bawden Drilling?" Reid screamed again, his voice now cracking from the smoke he breathed.

A few feet away from Reid, invisible in the murk, driller Fred Busby was splayed on the floor losing consciousness and unable to speak. With the help of an unseen arm pulling him to his feet, Busby got up and staggered toward the exit to the outside staircase. Finally, a flashlight beam found Reid, washing over his face like a slap.

"Over here. Here," rasped Jeff Jones, another driller who had just helped Busby get off the floor and moving. Jones was on his feet. Reid fell into arms. Jones shook Reid by the shoulders, looked him full in the face from a foot away, and said, "We have to get out of here or we're going to die. Do you understand?"

Reid nodded. He and Jones picked their way across men lying on the floor. Reid and Jones went through the kitchen, which was also packed with men, to a double door to the catwalk outside. Somebody lurched between them and the door. "You go out there, you're dead," he said. "It's fire everywhere."

"If we stay here, we're dead anyway," Jones said. "We've got nothing to lose."

Outside, Reid and Jones found themselves sheltered by a freight container the cooks used for storing meat and vegetables. Flames rose around them from the production modules below, but the con-

tainer blocked the worst of it. They felt their skin tighten against
the heat as they worked their way around to the open door facing away from the flames. It was impossible to see who was inside,
but somebody passed each of them a handful of ripe, red tomatoes.
Jones looked at his like he was staring at the strangest thing he had
ever seen. Reid didn't hesitate. He slapped the tomatoes on top of
his head and gained a moment's relief from their moisture dripping
down his face. Jones looked at him and smashed his tomatoes on
his own head. Reid was stunned by how little heroism there was in
his moment of death, how wretched it was. Silently, he vowed not
to die there.

While Mark Reid rallied, Bob Ballantyne, Ian Gillanders, and Charlie McLaughlin left their stateroom after the shower collapsed and
took a circuitous route to the canteen through the warren of decks
and corridors in the accommodation module. They banged on doors
to awake anyone who was asleep and shouted, "Fire. Fire. Get up."
Along the way, they roused ten men who trailed behind them. When
they reached an exterior door, whoever was in the lead carefully
felt the steel. Most of the doors were hot to the touch so they left
them closed. As Ballantyne burst into the reception area outside the
canteen, he looked at his watch. Twenty minutes had passed since
the rig shuddered and the shower wall in his cabin fell on Gillanders. When a helicopter landed, the noise in the accommodation was
loud enough to stop conversation. Ballantyne had heard nothing.
Tharos's chopper would have taken no more than six or seven minutes to reach Piper Alpha, but the fire and smoke drove it away. If
Tharos's chopper couldn't land, neither could any other helicopters.
Ballantyne knew there was no chance for evacuation by air.

From the stairway in the reception area, Ballantyne heard
screams and hollers coming from the canteen. Someone sobbed
in the darkness, a guttural wail so theatrical that Ballantyne had
a hard time believing it was real. There was no hope if he went
in there. As he stood wondering where to go, the Tartan pipeline
blew up, sending a pulse of heat that turned the stairway into an

inferno. Ballantyne thought about his choices. Up. Down. Going up was definitely out because there were no choppers landing. If he was going to jump off the rig, he was better off getting as close to the sea as he could before he did it. He turned to find Gillanders and McLaughlin and saw them heading toward the stairway down. Ballantyne followed them. He sidestepped through clutches of men sitting patiently on the stairs awaiting orders, slapping each one of them as he passed and motioning them to follow him. None of them moved, a few swatted at Ballantyne's hand as though he had committed some indiscretion by urging them to flee. One deck down, Ballantyne found the doorway out to the catwalk on the south side of the accommodation module. The door didn't feel too hot. If he found a clear way down, he thought, he would return to the canteen and lead the others to safety. From the catwalk, he saw that the core of the rig below him was disintegrating. He saw heavy steel valves and the blowout preventers on the wellheads sagging out of shape and thought for an instant of Salvador Dali's bizarre painting of the melting watch. The horror of the fire froze him for a moment. A clump of fire, as big and tidy as a beach ball, blew past him into the sky, singeing his hair and eyebrows as it passed. Finally, as though he was moving in a dream, Ballantyne ran for the only open air he could see on the east end of the catwalk. There was a long stairway down to the pipe deck, a sixty-by-sixty-foot open area thirty feet below where drill pipe was stored. If he jumped from the pipe deck, 130 feet above the sea, he had a chance to survive. He might also be able to work his way even lower on the rig.

At about that time, Bill Barron also realized that the canteen was a death trap. He and Barry Goodwin got as far as the stairway leading to the reception area and saw that the smoke was getting worse the higher up on the rig they went. Barron had been deeply conditioned to follow orders to assemble in the canteen in an emergency. Going against his training was not an easy decision. As he stood at the bottom of the stairs, he was also torn because so few others in the canteen were fleeing on their own. He wanted to take them with him and thought of going back.

Goodwin interrupted Barron's indecision. "Willie. We've got to

get off this fucking rig. Down is the only way." They bolted for the
same door through which Ballantyne had passed a minute earlier,
heading for the pipe deck.

At the freight container twenty feet from where Barron and Goodwin fled the accommodation module, Mark Reid and Jeff Jones collapsed with a dozen other men against the side of the container.
The tomatoes were all gone and with them all hope of relief. The
air seemed to be just a little clearer there, though the fire was still
roaring past them from the center of the rig. Maybe the choppers
had a shot after all. Reid got to his feet and wobbled to the edge of
the catwalk from where he could see the helideck twenty feet above
him. There were men up there. One of them, another driller named
Doug Findlay, shouted down, "You can catch your breath up here.
The air's pretty clear. Not so much smoke now."

Reid waved.

"Not me," Jones said. "I'm going down."

The fire below seemed impenetrable when Reid looked over the
rail and considered his next move. He glanced across the catwalk to
the south corner of the deck at the tanks for aviation fuel. The wind
could shift in a heartbeat and bring the fire to ignite them. He had
to go somewhere. Anywhere was better than where he was. Up, he
thought. I've got to go up. Reid stood painfully. For the first time,
he felt the burning.

All over Piper Alpha, the men who were still alive faced the same
choices. Obey training and stay put. Disobey and go down. In the
canteen, Jimmy McDonald, a rigger, asked an Occidental boss for
instructions. The boss said something that sounded like "Don't
worry, we're getting there, we're getting there," and babbled into
incoherence.

McDonald said aloud to himself, "Get yourself off." He grabbed
another rigger who was crouching next to him and dragged him
toward the reception area. At the door, the rigger pulled back into
the canteen.

"We have done our muster job. They'll send choppers in," the
rigger said.

McDonald yelled into his friend's face, "I've tried to speak to a boss. He talked gibberish to me. There's something drastically wrong on this rig. We have to get off."

The rigger pushed McDonald away and slumped to the floor.

For many, the decisions were made by the fire above or below them, something nobody had ever seen before. The true nature of fire was so alien to them that it was able to defeat their will to survive. On the drill floor, the Bawden men on the night shift had been driving wedges into the top of the well to keep the pipe from slipping down. They were directly below the inferno on the sixty-eight-foot level and the production deck. For them, there was no choice but to go down.

Far above, at the top of the rig in the shambles of Piper Alpha's radio room, David Kinrade transmitted Maydays on emergency batteries. He fought off the heat until he could stand it no longer. He was dazed, but fiercely aware that saving the men on his rig with a final desperate call for help was worth his own life. With the last of his courage, Kinrade made a final plea, speaking with the breathless clarity of a man who might be saying his last words.

"People majority in canteen area. *Tharos* come. Gangway. Hoses. Getting bad."

Twelve

THAROS

Shortly after ten that night, Captain Alastair Letty had been set-tling into sleep aboard *Tharos* when the alarm bell broke through the ordinary hum of machinery and woke him up. He was out of his bunk and on his feet by the time two quick knocks hit the cabin door. His first mate, Tony Ashby, looked in and said, "Piper's on fire."

Letty had swept aside the curtains over his porthole. He and *Tharos* had been hovering around Piper Alpha long enough to know that the flames he saw were coming from the production deck. Gas, Letty thought. The fire didn't look too bad, but there was no ques-tion that he had to maneuver *Tharos* close enough to ratchet out its steel gangway in case of an evacuation. The gangway was fully retracted. It would take at least an hour to extend it to its full length of 120 feet across open water to the stricken rig. At the moment, he loathed the truth about the ship he commanded. *Tharos* had been built to tend to the aftermath of an oil rig explosion by capping a runaway well on the bottom of the ocean, not to pluck terrified men from a burning rig when their lives were measured in minutes instead of hours.

Letty looked at Ashby with the inquisitive expression of a ship's captain who expected his subordinates to read his mind. He was the master of one of the most unusual vessels on earth, but he was still a forty-two-year-old Devonshire mariner with instincts rooted in a thousand years of British seafaring.

"We're paying out cable," Ashby told him.

Letty told Ashby to stay on duty in the front control room, get

Tharos's Sikorsky S-76 helicopter into the air immediately, and launch the Z-boat. The twelve-passenger Sikorsky was stationed on *Tharos* as a shuttle chopper. It didn't have a hoisting winch for at-sea rescue, so it would have to land on Piper Alpha to pick up survivors. If it couldn't land, the Z-boat would be hunting for men from the sea. For the first time in four years, Letty, Ashby, and the forty-man crew of *Tharos* were going to see action.

Armand Hammer had built *Tharos* at the Mitsubishi shipyard in Japan ten years earlier at a cost of $100 million. He was riding a crest of success that convinced him that he could turn Occidental Petroleum into the most profitable offshore oil company on earth. The profits from the Piper Field were exceeding his wildest expectations. If all else failed, *Tharos* was equipped not only as a firefighter and hospital but also as a self-sufficient drilling machine that could operate in any ocean. The future of petroleum exploration and extraction was clearly in deeper and deeper waters, and the company Hammer had built was going to lead the way. In 1980, Prince Philip, the Duke of Edinburgh, attended the flag-raising ceremony when *Tharos* went to work on the North Sea. After ten years in business together, the prince and Hammer were friends. In a television interview the following day, the prince called *Tharos* the world's most expensive fire engine. It was a tribute, he said, to the ingenuity and concern for safety shared by all companies in the North Sea. Occidental's in-house newsletter said it had been built "to fight fires, kill oil wells, and provide support and hospital facilities during any offshore emergency."

Hammer had called on the legendary oil field fire-fighter Paul "Red" Adair to help design *Tharos*. Adair had given the oil business its first classical hero when John Wayne played him in the 1968 movie *Hellfighters*. The film assured audiences that no matter how bad things got, if an oil well exploded, there was someone who could fix it. Adair had put out oil well fires in Libya and Texas for Hammer, who considered him a friend. Both men were of a type, self-made, rich, and bold—qualities that would have repelled them from each other if they had been competitors but which bonded them as mutually dependent. Adair was the son of an immigrant Irish blacksmith who went to work in the oil fields around Houston during the Depression and found his perfect career. When a valve blew out on the well he was working on, everybody ran for cover except him. He had been on a bomb disposal squad in the First World War and the fire just didn't scare him. Adair studied the situation and instinctively understood that if he could deprive the fire of oxygen it would go out. He put a keg of dynamite on a crane cable, swung it over the roaring column of flame, the keg blew up, and the fire was out. For the next fifty years, Adair made millions putting out oil rig fires.

Tharos was legally a ship, subject to maritime law, able to move under its own power, which differentiated it from a barge. Its crew had signed ship's articles as they would have coming aboard a tanker, freighter, or cruise liner. *Tharos*'s similarities to what most people thought of as a seafaring craft ended there, but the strange contraption was an engineering masterpiece. It was the size of five football fields side by side, weighing 30,000 tons, fixed to a pair of submerged pontoons by eight steel columns. It could move at seven knots driven by six 3,600 horsepower diesels, anchor in water a mile deep, and hold position precisely in winds up to gale force using nine 2,400 horsepower thrusters controlled by a computer on the bridge. Tanks in its hull and pontoons could hold eight million gallons of ballast, fuel, water, drilling mud, and concrete, giving *Tharos* a maximum draft under load or ballast of eighty-two feet— equivalent to a ten-story building. Three decks of accommodation modules on *Tharos* could hold up to three hundred men rescued from a stricken rig, topped by a helideck, a hangar for the Sikorsky, and davits for ten of the best lifeboats money could buy. On the working deck, *Tharos* had a three-hundred-ton crane, a drilling derrick for clearing and capping wells, and sixteen water cannons designed by Red Adair emplaced around the perimeter of the platform. Each cannon could pump forty thousand gallons of water per minute over a distance of 240 feet. They were so powerful that in a tight stream, the water could cut steel. Their crews were trained to shoot the water in arcing cascades to avoid maiming any men who were aboard a stricken rig. Except for the rare occasions when *Tharos* was a fire engine, it was a research and development tool for learning how to drill wells and lay pipelines in deep water. It had decompression chambers, pumps, equipment shops, television cameras, and robot arms that maneuvered at the end of tethers, and a revolutionary diving bell that allowed divers to work for up to a month at depths down to twelve hundred feet. In good weather, *Tharos* could be linked to Piper Alpha by its gangway as a floating hotel when extra men were offshore for maintenance or construction. In the summer of 1982, the sea went from flat calm to a ten-foot swell in a matter of minutes, the gangway collapsed, and three men died. Only once before, when Piper Alpha's gas storage tanks exploded in 1984 had the world's most expensive fire engine been pressed into service. Then, 220 evacuees were safely shuttled from the smoldering rig by helicopter.

After seeing the first flames erupt twenty minutes earlier on Piper Alpha, *Tharos*'s First Mate Ashby had pressed a button on the ship's intercom and said, "Hands to emergency stations. Fire on the rig. Fire on the rig." Medic David Olley, an oil field veteran who had worked in Libya, Norway, and Arabia, bolted from his stateroom. Five minutes after the alarm sounded, he had assembled his squad of cooks and stewards to prepare the hospital to receive injured men. *Tharos* could handle twenty-two injured men at a time in a six-bed sick bay connected to four four-berth staterooms. In each stateroom, Olley and his crew hung IV bottles of saline, prepared trays with injections of Demerol for pain, and set up oxygen lines from tanks buckled onto the walls. After triage, stabilized or dying men would be moved to other staterooms to await evacuation to shore by helicopter. Some of Olley's men went to *Tharos*'s cinema in the accommodation module where they set up more IVs, portable oxygen, and first-aid kits to treat men with minor injuries.

While Olley worked, he went through mental checklists to prepare himself for the kinds of injuries he was most likely to see. Oil rigs were really just big factories, dangerous assemblages of heavy steel that broke, fell, and twisted, and machines that were capable of crushing and tearing flesh and bone with indifference to the lives of workingmen. Their drills, chains, and howling machinery had the power to wound in return for a slight misstep, to utterly demolish a human body for grave error. Industrial lore in the oil business is replete with stories about accidents in which the victims were reduced to pink vapor or unrecognizable smudges in the machines.

Worst of all, the oil and gas that filled the tanks, pipes, and pumps on oil rigs could inflict terrible burns when ignited. Olley was an emergency medical technician. He had been taught that his first decision about a burned man was whether or not the victim had a chance to live. Skin is the largest single organ in a human body, a layered, self-replenishing miracle of specialized cells that regulates temperature, secretes fluids, and protects the more fragile cells within from trauma. It is the most easily assaulted by fire simply because it is on the outside of the body. The depth of that assault and the amount of the skin that has been burned were the criteria on which Olley had to make his decisions. Slight pain, itching, and redness meant the burns were first degree, not much more than the penalty paid for a day at the beach without sunscreen. If the skin was blistered, the burns were second degree. They penetrated the first layer of skin, were extremely painful and susceptible to infection, but they were not life-threatening. Third-degree burns destroyed both layers of skin and ate into the bones, blood vessels, and organs beneath them, leaving pale, charred, or leathery tissue on the surface. A person with third-degree burns usually felt very little pain because the fire killed nerve endings. A man could be burned beyond hope and still be alive to know it. If a burn victim had a chance to survive, Olley's job was to keep him from dehydrating with intravenous fluids, keep his airway open, administer Demerol for pain, and coat the skin with ointments to protect it from infection. If a victim had third-degree burns over more than half his body, he was almost certain to die. His body would collapse into shock and a cascade of organ failure from which it could not recover. Olley's ministrations, he knew, would be palliative. His words to the victim carefully spoken to conceal the inevitable.

It took Olley fifteen minutes to finish his preparations. After a final pass through the sick bay, he went outside to get some idea of how bad the fire was and how many men would be coming aboard. When the alarm rang, he had hurried to the sick bay from his cabin without going outside. Olley expected to see a few wisps of smoke coming from the rig, evidence of a manageable problem. He clanked up the metal stairway from the sick bay, threw the toggle handles on a watertight door, and stepped out on deck. The entire middle of Piper Alpha was on fire. The flames dwarfed the still burning gas flare booms at the east and west corners. As he watched, a roaring ball of flame detached itself from the rig and rolled into the sky, trailing a dense column of black smoke. In another few seconds, the fire settled back to retake the rig. He saw but couldn't hear *Tharos*'s Sikorsky fleeing the conflagration as the fire reached up to Piper Alpha's accommodation module and the helideck above it.

Nobody can be alive, Olley thought.

On *Tharos*'s bridge, Captain Letty stood over his propulsion controls and barked orders through the intercom to the winch men who were on deck paying out anchor cable. His plan was to shield his approach with the deluge from his water cannons, and get the gangway out as far as he could in the time it took him to get to the rig. His Z-boat was already in the water thanks to Ashby's quick reaction. He wasn't sure what was going on with the Sikorsky. He set that thought aside when the radio crackled with a call from Piper Alpha.

"People majority in canteen area. *Tharos* come. Gangway. Hoses. Getting bad."

Letty and *Tharos* were still a quarter mile away. He was deep in the water, ballasted for stability. Under those conditions, he could only make two knots, not even the speed of a walking man. The chopper, Letty thought. He snatched his intercom mike and calmly requested a status report on the Sikorsky from the helideck. His helicopter landing boss, a usually unflappable pro, sounded like a witness to a car crash.

"The helo is airborne. A Module is on fire. B Module is on fire. C Module is on fire. They have fire from water level to the helideck. In fact, the whole fucking thing is on fire."

Thirteen

ESCAPE

Ed Punchard, Stan McCleod, Gareth Parry-Davies, and four other men shinnied down a knotted rope from the navigation platform. They picked their way along the oil-slick steel gratings of the spider deck to a ladder on the rig's northwest leg where they would either be safe until help arrived or jump twenty feet into the sea. They had seen the underside of Piper Alpha countless times, but now it seemed alien to them as they ran. Toward the center of the rig, they looked through a forest of pipes, the thirty-six well casings, the bigger risers from Tartan, Claymore, and MCP-01, the unfinished Chanter riser, and the thirty-inch main oil pipeline. They could see fire and smoke seeping down the channels through which the pipes descended from the deck above them. Below them, the water sloshed against the pipes where they entered the sea in a dissonant chorale like a huge, basso wind chime. The much larger legs and cross-braces of the rig were flat yellow in the dim light, fading instantly to nothing where they disappeared into the sea on their long descent to the bottom.

Next to the northwest leg, a twenty-foot-high tube of vulcanized rubber was welded to the rig as a bumper for supply boats that sometimes unloaded there. Beneath the men, the water reflected the dark smoke billowing out at an angle to the northeast. Their escape route was clear, except for wisps of smoke blown under the rig by back eddies. Against a faint blue twilight sky, lit by the orange tongue of flame on the flare boom, the folds and creases in the billowing smoke looked like pulsing veins.

The dash to the northwest leg took a little over a minute. From the top of the ladder, the men saw the dark shape of *Silver Pit* jogging about a hundred yards away to the left. As though on cue, they all shouted, waved, and pointed to the boat bumper next to the leg. Someone on the bridge wing of *Silver Pit* waved back and pointed down to the water. The banshee wail of a high-powered engine overcame the noise of the fire and the sea as a Z-boat sped into view heading for the bottom of the ladder.

The crew of the twenty-four-foot Z-Boat wore orange survival suits and white helmets, the coxswain at the steering wheel in the middle of the boat, two others sitting abreast behind him. Under ordinary circumstances, the mariners on the oil field boats and the men who worked on North Sea rigs treated each other with the mutual condescension typical among members of different military services. The mariners thought the oil men were factory drones stupid enough to work in the most dangerous factories on earth. The oil men thought the mariners were incompetent, rootless wanderers who were always slamming into the rigs or refusing to unload cargo in less-than-perfect sea conditions. As the Z-boat nuzzled up to the bottom of the ladder and swung its stern against the rubber bumper, all that tribal antagonism vanished. From Piper Alpha, the men gazed down at their saviors. On the Z-boat, coxswain James McNeill, Charles Haffey, and Andy Kiloh looked up at the knot of frantically waving men and knew that they were performing the most important and heroic act of their lives.

McNeill and his crew had already saved one man. As they sped away from *Silver Pit* on their first run to the rig, a human silhouette against the glowing fire waved frantically to them from one of the boarding ladders on the spider deck. Mahmood Khan, a chemist, had been working in the oil lab on the drill floor when the explosion knocked him off his feet. He stuck his head out the door, saw fire and smoke above him, and knew he couldn't get through it to the lifeboats or the canteen. When Khan climbed down the ladder into the Z-boat, he was unhurt but trembling so badly that McNeill decided to take him straight back to *Silver Pit*. McNeill had seen men in fire suits and breathing gear on Piper Alpha's production deck. If they were fighting the blaze, they might soon have things under control. He figured he could afford the time it took to get the babbling Khan to the ship. Haffey tried to calm down the terrified chemist with talk of a cup of tea and a warm bed on *Silver Pit*.

In the precious minutes it took McNeill to drop off Khan and turn his Z-boat back for a second run, fire and smoke took over of the middle decks of the rig. McNeill had been in the navy during the Falklands War. He had seen a warship on fire—HMS *Sheffield*—but nothing like the inferno on Piper Alpha. Above him, men materialized like backlit shadow puppets at the edges of the rig. Some retreated. Some jumped. One of them plunged from eighty feet up into the sea, trailing flames from his back. McNeill turned for an instant toward the point at which the burning man hit the water. At the edge of his vision, he saw what looked like a dozen or more men clustered and waving next to the boat bumper at the northwest leg. Save the most, McNeill thought. He knew then that he would be living for the rest of his life with the regrets for many of the choices he was going to make that night. He steered toward the northwest leg. In the light swell, he had no trouble maneuvering. It was about a two-foot hump, no white caps, no sharp troughs. The only real danger was being pushed under the rig where he could see debris in the water that might puncture the boat with sharp steel edges. McNeill reversed the engine as his boat nosed into the leg, felt a little bounce as it struck, then held it steady with a touch of forward thrust. Haffey and Kiloh were already in the bow, their hands reaching up to guide the stricken men. McNeill counted nine, gauging the loading of his boat. He could take them all in one trip.

Punchard happened to be the closest man to the top of the ladder when *Silver Pit*'s Z-boat arrived. He was the first to descend, swinging over the rail from the spider deck, feeling his hand clench on the top rung as though his mind was willing him to stay and help, or stay and die, or just to stay with the men who were not getting off. He hadn't seen his roommate, who was the dive team photo tech and who had run upstairs to call his wife just before the explosion. Barry Barber was still missing. So were all the day shift divers. Punchard felt a bolt of regret. He might be the first man off the burning rig. It felt ignoble. He was going to survive, to remain available to his dream of exploring ancient shipwrecks and living in a tropical paradise with a beautiful wife and pretty little daughter. Men he knew like brothers would not. Punchard lurched down the ladder until Haffey and Kiloh took his arms and peeled him off the rig.

"I'm okay. I'm okay," Punchard said, turning to help the men behind him until Haffey pushed him toward the stern. As he slipped past the steering console, McNeill asked if he was hurt. In that moment, shock claimed Punchard, lifting him into a daze in which he felt like a little kid in a forbidden place where he was not supposed to be. He shook his head, slouched against the towing platform at the back of the boat, and gazed numbly at the ships scuttling around the rig in the glow of the weird orange light.

The *Maersk Cutter* was three hundred feet off the northeast corner of Piper Alpha. Ten minutes after the first explosion, her water cannons were pumping seventy-five hundred gallons a minute onto the drilling floor on the south end, most of which vaporized as the intensity of the fire increased.

The *Lowland Cavalier* had drifted almost a mile downwind off the northwest corner. It had no water cannons, but its Z-boat was already speeding toward Piper Alpha. Captain Michael Clegg on *Cavalier*'s bridge watched helplessly through binoculars. He ordered his crew to man the rails with searchlights to watch for survivors and bodies carried toward them by the current.

The converted supply ship *Sandhaven* was four and a half miles away, on station as the standby boat for a floating drill rig exploring the fringes of the Piper Field. Its captain had his Z-boat in the water three minutes after he spotted the first fire on Piper Alpha. It was an Atlantic 21, an especially fast, gas-powered, rigid hull inflatable that could make thirty knots and took only five minutes to reach the burning rig. Ian Letham, Brian Batchelor, and Malcolm Storey were the crew, all of them ordinary seamen grateful to break the tedium of duty on a standby boat with a breakneck run to a rig in distress.

Six hundred feet west of Piper Alpha, the lumbering mass of *Tharos* edged painfully slowly toward the inferno. Captain Letty was almost blinded by the backwash from his own water cannons, which were firing but falling well short of the rig. Worried that he might collide with the rig's flare boom as he approached, he corrected his course to the center of the west face, which was completely engulfed in flames. His plan was to extend his aluminum gangway to the rig's eighty-three-foot level but he could see that the worst of the fire was burning right there. The gangway was still twenty-five minutes from full extension. There was no place where it could connect to the rig that was not on fire. The gangway was useless. Letty kept *Tharos* on course.

McNeill gunned his Z-boat clear of Piper Alpha's leg, alert to junk in the water and burning debris raining down from the rig. As the bow swung out toward *Silver Pit,* Punchard and the other survivors turned to look up at the rig from their seats in the stern. They were surprised that the rig was not completely on fire, though raging knots of flame erupted from the production deck immediately above the dive offices. Most dominant in the sky above them was a cloud of smoke, much blacker than the coming night, rising hundreds of feet from the center of the rig through the accommodation module and out to the north.

In less than a minute, McNeill reached *Silver Pit.* The only way onto the ship was a boarding net, draped over the side, which the men had to climb. Punchard was the last up, grabbing a handful of rope as McNeill spun the Z-boat out from under him and headed back to Piper Alpha. Arms reached down amid the men scrambling onto *Silver Pit*'s deck. The first nine came aboard. With Khan, who sat with a cup of tea on a hatch cover, the men awoke to the fact of their own survival. A hundred yards away, the fire on Piper Alpha was getting worse. They saw men everywhere, some climbing down ladders toward the sea, others running around in the smoke storm on the helideck. For the first time since descending from the navigation light platform, they spoke to each other expecting to be heard.

"Did you see what happened to Dick Common?" one of the divers asked Punchard. "He was climbing down the rope from the navigation platform we all came down. He let go of it and bounced off the boat bumper into the sea."

"I saw it," Punchard said. "That's the end of him." Punchard fought off his own gratitude for being alive, knowing that it could have easily been him and not Common losing his grip on the rope.

George Carson, *Silver Pit*'s medic, moved from man to man, checking them for wounds. Most were unhurt. He told one of his stewards to go to the bridge and bring the captain's medical box to the boarding deck. The first ten men who had reached *Silver Pit* were in good shape, but the holocaust above him was not going to spare many the agony of burns. They would need the morphine.

The Z-boat was back at *Silver Pit* four minutes later with another load of men, the faces of McNeill and his crew frozen into masks of stoic determination. Some of the men on *Silver Pit* who had been in the military recognized it as the thousand-yard stare they had seen before only in combat. Dick Common, soaking wet, was the first man over the side. Punchard was amazed, overcome with the hope that he had abandoned and found over and over again since he ran from the dive office. He was sure Common was dead. Common was a clerk, a slightly built man who looked like a tap on the shoulder would crumble him. In the dive office, he was an almost laughable counterpoint to the tough, muscled divers. Common looked shocky but alert. When Punchard grabbed his arm in a gesture of affection, he said he was fine. Carson came up, looked at Common's eyes, and asked him why he was wet. Common stammered out his story and told Carson he had hit the bumper with the small of his back, pulling up his shirt to show him where. There wasn't a mark on him.

"You had a lot of guts climbing down that rope," Punchard said, squeezing Common's shoulder.

"I didn't want to go, but Barry Barber said, 'Don't tell me it's fucking difficult. Get down that fucking rope.' So I set off."

Punchard inventoried the men around him, some silent, some jabbering to each other in bursts out of the sides of their mouths as they stared at Piper Alpha burning above them. Barry Barber was not on *Silver Pit*. Stan McCleod, standing next to Punchard, saw his friend's grief flow into his face and said, "I'm glad you got off, Ed." Gareth Parry-Davies walked from man to man, asking each, "Where's John Barr?" Punchard, who had been fading in and out of the daze into which he had fallen when he left the rig, snapped out of it by giving himself a job. Somebody had to keep track of the names of the survivors who came aboard. He knew he would soon be recording the names of the dead. Punchard trotted aft up the ladder to the bridge to fetch a pen and paper. In the wheelhouse, *Silver Pit*'s captain, John Sabourn, acknowledged him with a nod and turned away, struck dumb by the escalating horror around him.

Sabourn had allowed his ship to drift on the northerly current to within two hundred feet of Piper Alpha. He couldn't risk pulling up to a boarding ladder on the rig, but his Z-boat could make faster round-trips if he was closer. If there were men swimming in the water, they would have less distance to cover. *Silver Pit* was not built for close-in maneuvering. She had a single engine, a small rudder, and a bow thruster that hadn't worked at all since leaving Aberdeen a few days earlier. Sabourn, who had commanded many ships that were not forty-year-old converted fishing trawlers, compared docking *Silver Pit* to driving a bus from the backseat with the side windows blacked out.

Maneuverability wasn't Sabourn's only problem. The searchlight on the bridge wasn't working and there were no spare bulbs. As the Z-boat returned with its third load, the only illumination was from deck lights, flashlights, and the burning rig itself. Sabourn looked down from the wheelhouse through the dirty orange glow and saw one of his crew trying to launch *Silver Pit*'s second rescue boat, a smaller inflatable with an outboard motor that would not start. Worst of all, the boarding net was ludicrous. Many survivors were burned or cut so badly that they screamed with pain while climbing aboard. In twenty minutes, there were fifteen or twenty men standing or lying around on the deck. Carson had managed to get three with bad burns into the sick bay, which wasn't easy because of the narrow doors and passageways built for fishermen who could walk on their own power. The medic had paid close attention during his two-day EMT training course when he took the job on *Silver Pit*, but he felt helpless to do much except keep the wounded calm. He used his first morphine syrette on a man who was in deep shock and unaware that the entire back of his head was charred with the white of his skull showing through.

At twenty-two minutes past ten, the valves at the top of the Tartan gas pipeline on Piper Alpha liquefied and released the force of billions of highly explosive molecules of gas into fire. What had been an emergency on an oil rig to which *Silver Pit,* her Z-boat, and crew were responding became a threat to their own survival. A bolt of bluish yellow flame shot straight up into the sky, then collapsed onto itself in a roiling ball that completely engulfed the rig. The *Maersk Cutter* and the *Lowland Cavalier* came into sharper focus as the inferno turned night to day, both of them visibly shuddering as the blast rolled over them. On *Tharos*'s bridge, Captain Letty commanded all stop as the momentum of his massive vessel carried it closer and closer to the flames. *Tharos* was within water cannon range, but the arcs she was throwing on the fire vaporized before they reached the rig.

Sixty feet above the sea on the navigation platform, Bob Ballantyne lost sight of Ian Gillanders and Charlie McLaughlin when he fled from the canteen. After a dash across the pipe deck and down to the navigation light platform on the southwest corner of the spider deck, he spotted Gillanders and McLaughlin on the other side of the rig. He hollered, but they were oblivious, clinging to a ladder on the steel leg halfway between the spider deck and the water, waving frantically at a Z-boat that looked like its crew had seen them and was turning. As Ballantyne steeled himself for the jump, he noticed a rope tied to one of the rails, looked down, and saw its other end limp on the catwalk of the spider deck. He could easily climb down to the water from there. Somebody, Ballantyne thought, has given me a gift.

In the water, bobbing in his life vest, Ballantyne huddled against the leg of the rig, afraid to let go and be sucked into the flaming debris all around him. The water was warm. He felt himself lose his grip on the bottom rung of the ladder, spun out and away by an explosion that thudded into his body like a heavyweight boxer's punch. Ballantyne let go and began to drift as the water around him glowed with a fierce orange.

On *Silver Pit*'s deck, Ed Punchard watched the sky explode and slipped back into shock. "It's happened at last. How odd I should be here." He looked around at the two dozen or so men on deck with the sickening realization that they might be the only survivors.

Where was John Barr? Barry Barber? He saw no way that anyone still left on Piper Alpha could escape the inferno that blotted out every vestige of the former world, no way anyone could survive the flames.

Stan McCleod took charge of pulling men up the rope net and keeping the other divers at the rails facing the rig to spot men in the water. Against the stygian glow of the sea, shapes materialized everywhere, some of them indecipherable hunks of floating debris, others clearly men struggling to stay afloat. Punchard, who was second-in-command, hollered up to the bridge for Captain Sabourn to steer closer to Piper Alpha. Sabourn yelled back that he couldn't risk hitting them with his prop but the current was bringing him closer anyway. Several times, *Silver Pit* drew near to something in the water and without its own power drifted past. Parry-Davies ran up to Punchard and pointed down at what looked like pieces of a lifeboat or a big box to which three or four men were clinging.

"We've got to get those guys," Parry-Davies shouted. He was still in his diving suit. "Tell that fucking idiot on the bridge I'm going to leap into the sea and get those guys. Just make sure he knows what I'm doing." Parry-Davies tied a docking line around his waist and jumped over the side. As soon as he was in the water, he saw that one man on a single piece of debris had drifted into the lee of *Silver Pit* and kicked toward him.

Punchard ran to the bridge to tell Sabourn what was happening. "We've got a diver in the water," he yelled over the roar of the fire. "He's off the port side, fifteen feet away. Don't turn the prop." Below him in the water, Punchard saw Parry-Davies stop swimming, turn to the ship, and wave his arms. He was at the end of his rope. Punchard yelled down to find more rope and tie it on. Everyone on deck who was able to walk looked unsuccessfully for more rope. In the water, Parry-Davies bellowed and splashed as the man he might have saved drifted away.

Fourteen

HELL

After the Tartan gas pipeline exploded, Bill Barron and Barry Goodwin heard the sinister crack of breaking glass and the howls of men fighting off the heat in the galley and fled the accommodation module. On the catwalk outside, they saw others huddled in the fire shadow of the cooks' refrigerated container, smashing fruit on their heads. Below them, the edge of the production deck around the lifeboats was completely engulfed in flame. Above, on the helideck, fire and smoke enveloped the precious landing pad the helicopters needed to rescue them. The noise was deafening, the air suffocating and thick with the aroma of burnt rubber and a sharp chemical odor. As the painting boss, Barron knew every inch of Piper Alpha. He could move around the rig with his eyes closed. The wind and whatever was fueling the fire below him were carrying most of the flame across the rig from west to east, leaving what looked like an opening on the pipe deck thirty feet below. There was smoke between him and the ladder down, but running into it was worth the risk. Barron yelled over his shoulder to Goodwin. "The pipe deck. The pipe deck." Goodwin nodded and clapped Barron on the back. They descended into the noxious cloud.

Seconds later, they were ten feet down the ladder in mercifully clear air. Barron was right. The pipe deck was open. Most of the smoke rising from it was coming from burning hydraulic fluid pouring out of a crane. The worst fire was on the other side of the rig. To their right, toward the interior of the rig, the flames were the worst. They kept to the outer edge of the deck and worked their way to the ladder down to the drilling floor, turning their faces and palms

upward as they ran to catch miraculous droplets of cooling water
that were coming from somewhere. At the top of the next ladder,
Barron and Goodwin pulled up short. From the direction of the
tool shed known as the White House forty feet away on the other
side of the pipe deck, they heard measured cries for help and pan-
icked screaming. Barron had a man working on that side of the rig
before the fire started. Most of his painting crew were taking time
off while they waited for the Chanter riser to be finished, but he
had given one young fellow some overtime doing an easy inside job.
Barron barely knew the kid, but he was just married and needed
money so he helped him out. Leaving Goodwin at the top of the
ladder, Barron took a few steps in the direction of the White House
before Goodwin grabbed his arm and pulled him back. "You can't
do anything, Willie. Not a goddamn thing," Goodwin yelled.

Barron and Goodwin clanged down onto the southwest edge of
the drill floor, which was smoky but not unbearably hot. Still too
high. They got under the sixty-eight-foot level where the flames were
an absolute wall to the north and east of them and reached a navigation light platform on the leg of the rig. They were sixty feet from
the sea. From somewhere above, a man flew past them through the
air, hit the water, and vanished in the center of a splash tinged ocher
by the fire above. For long seconds, Barron froze at the rail, looking
down where the man had gone in, waiting for him to surface. One
of the little Z-boats buzzing around the base of the rig darted in the
direction of the fallen man just under where they were standing.

Goodwin slapped Barron's shoulder and handed him a coil of
inch-and-a-half docking rope. "Go, Willie," Goodwin yelled. Barron looked at his friend, smiled, and said, "I can't swim, Barry. I
can't fucking swim. You go first. I'll hang on to the rope until the
boat is closer."

Goodwin was a decent swimmer. Like Barron, he was wearing
a life vest. It was a good plan. Goodwin took back the coil of rope,
checked to be sure it was fast to a cleat on the platform, and let it
unfurl. The bitter end was only fifteen feet above the water. Behind
him, Goodwin felt a rush of hot wind that singed his hair. He knew
he wouldn't get another chance and went over the rail. At first he
held on too tight and just hung there, feeling the rope swaying in

the wind from the center of the rig. He eased his grip, feeling the bristly burn of the rope sliding through his hands, and hit the knot at the bottom before he was ready for it. Goodwin fell, the sea close enough now to remind him of jumps he had made into quarries as a kid. It didn't hurt when he hit and the water didn't even feel cold. He looked up, and there was Barron already at the end of the rope, his knees tucked to his chest as though cringing from the sea below him. Goodwin felt the current pushing him back under the rig, looked up and saw pieces of flaming junk raining down. He swam as hard as he could for open water. From the rope, Barron watched Goodwin stroking furiously away and saw the nose of the Z-boat pitch down abruptly as it lurched to a stop next to his friend. Close enough. Barron let go of the rope. He hit feet-first, but even with the life vest he submerged completely, sucking water into his lungs with the involuntary gasp of impact. Seconds later, he popped to the surface, dazed and coughing with his head forced back by the buoyancy of the vest so he was looking straight up at the worst thing he had ever seen. For a man working offshore, the rig was his safe haven, the only protection he had from a hostile ocean that at every moment threatened to dismantle his refuge. Piper Alpha was on fire, shedding pieces of itself into the sea. The current swung him around to face the miraculous orange pontoon of a Z-boat, and Barron knew he was saved. He felt the rough but blessed tug of a boat hook on his life vest as two men pulled him out of the ocean and back into life.

A half hour after the Tartan riser blew, the pipeline that connected Piper Alpha to the MCP-01 pumping platform in the Frigg gas field succumbed to the heat and exploded. It was a foot and a half in diameter, ran thirty-four miles northwest on the seafloor, and contained within that length 51 million cubic feet of explosive pressurized gas. A massive steel valve was fitted to the end of the pipeline on Piper Alpha to prevent a blowout. For almost a half hour, that valve had resisted the inferno fed by the Tartan riser. At 1,300 degrees Fahrenheit, it could no longer contain the gas. The two explosions that had gone before the ignition of the MCP-01 pipeline paled by comparison. A fireball a quarter mile in diameter bulged horizontally through the sixty-eight-foot level and the production deck above it, collapsing on itself as it consumed the oxygen it needed for ignition. In a microsecond, the fire caught its breath and erupted through Piper Alpha's upper decks and a half mile into the night sky, forming a huge mushroom cloud. The blast rattled the windows on every ship and oil rig within fifty miles. A false dawn startled thousands of people on the northeast coast of Scotland 130 miles away.

On *Silver Pit*, Captain John Sabourn looked at the chronometer on the wall of his bridge at the exact moment black-orange fire consumed the world around him: 10:52. He was 150 feet from Piper Alpha. The blast shook his ship as though it had run full speed into a jetty. In an instant, the air in the wheelhouse was hot enough to curl the charts on his plotting table. Sabourn raced to the bridge door and saw his Z-boat tearing away from the loading net on its way back to Piper Alpha. The fireball illuminated the scene like it was daylight, bursting from the platform in all directions and roaring three thousand feet into the sky. The plume of roiling smoke that had dominated the rig was now banished by a sheet of flame. On the bulkhead outside the bridge door, the paint blackened and crinkled, chips of it igniting and falling to the deck. Sabourn's mariner's instincts commanded him to save his ship. He took three strides back to his helm, threw *Silver Pit* into gear, and steered away from Piper Alpha.

For the first seconds after the MCP-01 pipeline blew, Ed Punchard was not aware of the heat on *Silver Pit*'s deck. Then he was. A scorching wind hit him as though he were standing in front of the open door of a steel mill furnace, a wind that carried the noxious aromas of burning paint, molten steel, and chemicals he had never smelled before. *Silver Pit* was so close to the blast that the oxygen content of the air Punchard was breathing plunged as the combustion devoured the air around him. A coil of rope on the deck at his feet began to smolder. Punchard saw some men escape the heat behind the stairway leading up to the bridge, but there was no more room there. He realized that he was going to be roasted alive if he stayed where he was. In two steps, Punchard was over the side, clinging to the rope boarding net on the side of the ship facing away from the inferno. Shelter. Beside him, Mahmood Khan made the same decision to leave the deck rather than risk the fire. Punchard was low on the net with his feet in the water, Khan above him. *Silver Pit* began to move. Of course, Punchard thought. Sabourn had no choice. As the ship gained momentum, Punchard's legs streamed aft, his feet still in his heavy, water-soaked rig boots.

Silver Pit was soon moving at six knots. Twice walking speed. Punchard felt his hands slipping off the rope net and forced himself to tighten his grip. Oh, hell, he thought. I'm not going to make it after all. For two minutes, he shouted as loudly as he could before a man wearing orange earmuffs looked down at him from the rail.

"Stop the ship," Punchard yelled.

Other heads appeared, including Stan McCleod looking at him like he was shocked to see a man being dragged through the water, but nobody did anything about it. Punchard fought to hold his head out of the water, gulping air and water, coughing. He heard the thrum and wash of the prop a few feet behind him and tightened his grip again. If he let go, he would be sucked into the blades and dead for sure. Even if he wasn't, there was a good chance that the current would carry him where nobody would find him. Punchard thought of Vicky and Suzie. He formed a clear picture of the two of them in his mind, and it gave him the strength to hold on for another minute. Khan clung to the rope above, flailing as he lost his foothold when *Silver Pit* gained speed. Now it was doing about ten knots. Punchard thought, they can't stop for two men and risk losing everybody else and the ship, too.

Parry-Davies appeared at the rail, waving his fist down at Punchard. "Fucking hang on. Fucking hang on."

A minute later, the prop behind Punchard was still and *Silver Pit* glided to a stop. Carrol and Parry-Davies kneeled at the top of the rope net and pulled Punchard to the deck. He was obsessed with getting his other boot off, yelling, "Get my boot off, get my boot off," completely ignoring the raging fire in the sky and the terror on the faces of the men looking down at him. The man in the orange earmuffs was beside him. George Carson, *Silver Pit*'s medic. "You're okay, Ed. You're okay," Carson said, kneeling at Punchard's side with his hand on his shoulder. "You're safe." Miraculously, Khan was alive and on deck, too.

Sabourn had steered *Silver Pit* in a wide arc away from the rig until he stopped again about a quarter mile off the northwest corner. Punchard staggered to his feet. What he saw buckled his knees again and he grabbed hold of the rail to stay upright. Piper Alpha was no longer an oil rig on fire; it was being consumed by the flames. From the spider deck downward, the steel was red-hot as though it were in a furnace. Beneath the rig, the water was steaming. The sky and the surrounding sea were bathed in a brilliant orange and the roar of the raging fire obliterated all other sounds. A thick pall of black smoke framed the hideous picture that fixed itself indelibly in Punchard's mind. He heard someone standing next to him say, "There's nothing left. Nobody left."

On *Tharos*, Captain Alistair Letty held his position five hundred feet from Piper Alpha. When the MCP-01 riser blew, he had a handheld radio to each ear, listening on one to the voice of his chopper pilot and on the other to a voice broadcast from Occidental headquarters in Aberdeen. From the pilot came a carefully modulated assessment of the conditions on Piper Alpha's helideck that continued to prohibit him from landing, wrought with the tension of fighting the controls as the blast buffeted the helicopter. "No chance, no chance, no chance," the pilot said. "Fire everywhere. No chance." In his other ear, Letty listened to a man at Oxy warning him he had to pull back from the burning rig because of the danger of deadly hydrogen sulfide. Letty was the captain of a ship at sea. Anything the man said was advisory and both knew it. *Tharos*'s Z-boat had made three runs into the inferno and returned with a dozen survivors. His water cannons were finally at full power, pumping thousands of gallons a minute into the inferno. There was no chance that he was going to get his gangway on the rig, but his ship was in no immediate danger. He decided to stay where he was unless it got worse.

In a metal fabrication shed on the pipe deck, Harry Calder and Ian Fowler prepared to die. Calder, a helicopter landing officer, had been wrapped in his blankets trying to sleep in his cabin on B Deck when he felt the rig shudder and pieces of the ceiling fall on the floor. Fowler, a joiner, had been in bed with his earphones on waiting for horse racing results on the late news. The two were friends from several tours on Piper Alpha and had hit the bars in Aberdeen together a few times. They were among the first men in the canteen after the explosion, dutifully obeying their orders to muster there in the event of emergency. Until the Tartan pipeline blew, Calder and Fowler believed that help was on the way. When the second wave of fire from the MCP-01 pipeline scalded the air, warmed the floor under their feet, and filled the canteen with smoke, they agreed to find safety on their own.

Some of the other men in the canteen who had made the same decision headed for the helicopter pad, the most obvious evacuation point with the lower decks aflame. Calder and Fowler went with them. Once there, they saw *Tharos*'s chopper in the air but hovering well away from Piper Alpha, making no attempt to land on the pad that was all but invisible in the smoke. After a moment's hesitation to see if the pad would clear, Calder and Fowler dashed down the ladder past the accommodation module and onto the side of the pipe deck that was on fire. They ran through a sliver of a corridor that opened in the flame and dashed for a ladder twenty feet away that would take them down. As they ran, the bullet-snaps of bursting equipment hoses and the roar of the burning pipeline in the center of the rig was deafening. Halfway to the down ladder, they knew they weren't going to make it. Calder pulled Fowler into a fabrication shed where they found another man sitting dazed and motionless on a chair in his red survival suit with a cloth pressed to his face. He looked like an exhibit in a wax museum, but nodded feebly to them with a look of resignation that was almost a smirk.

The shed was a twenty-by-thirty-foot metal hut in which the riggers, joiners, and drillers could get out of the weather while they patched together pipes and fittings. In the next minute, another ten men crowded in, some of them diving to the floor to escape the heat and smoke, others collapsing on pieces of equipment and boxes that had tumbled from racks on the walls. With the door closed, it was pitch-dark inside. Almost an hour had passed since the first explosion. The men had fled from places of certain death to places of less certain death, all the while with the expectation that where they were going was better than where they had been. In the fabrication shed, they knew they had reached the end. Around them, the roar of the fire was now punctuated by the groans and cracks of breaking steel, catwalks falling, pieces of deck plating separating and falling away. In the smoke-filled darkness, the men reached out to touch each other, some to embrace, some to shake hands. Most were crying, their sobs unrestrained by custom or pride. They said, "Goodbye," or "Well, this is it," or "This is the end." Under a steel table in the center of the room, Calder and Fowler threw their arms around each other. Calder turned away and vomited on the floor. Fowler said, "I'm passing out. I'm passing out." Calder recovered and said, "Come on, man." Calder stuck out his hand. "Goodbye, Ian. This is it." At that moment, the deck below them tore open with the shriek of tearing steel, giving them a clear view down to the water that looked like a burnt-orange sheet of rippling plastic. They were still 130 feet up, almost certain to die from the impact. After a heartbeat of hesitation, seeing only the flash of the fire on the water below, Calder and Fowler slid over the edge and let themselves fall into the North Sea.

The blast of the MCP-01 pipeline sent a shock wave through the water immediately below the rig, triggering a miniature tsunami. Bob Ballantyne, who had jumped into the water seconds before, was clinging to a steel ladder on one of the legs. The force of the explosion tore Ballantyne from the leg and propelled him a hundred feet downwind to the northwest, away from the worst of the fireball that followed the shock wave. As he crested a wave, he looked back and saw one of the Z-boats speeding from directly under the rig near where he had last seen Ian Gillanders and Charlie McLaughlin.

Good, Ballantyne thought. Good. They got off. In the next instant, the fireball expanded downward and vaporized the Z-boat, leaving no trace of it as the flame billowed out from under the rig and into the sky. Ballantyne had never seen anything like it, but he knew there was no hope for anyone in the boat. He began to scream, a raging, angry howl at the loss of his friends, at the filthy, miserable oil rig, at his own feeling of elation about being alive when the others were dead. Thank goodness I didn't make it to them, he thought. He felt no love or concern, only gratitude for his own survival. It sickened him.

Ballantyne was surrounded by a raft of floating sludge and the current was carrying him toward a patch of water that was actually on fire. His mind surprised him when it fell softly into a fantasy of the Clyde Football Club, his team, finally winning the European Cup. He thought of his sweetheart, Pat, and the three-week vacation to the south of France they were planning. The thought inspired him to kick away from the fire on the sea around him. Then came Amanda, his daughter. He had not seen her for six years, not since his divorce. He promised himself that he would hold her in his arms again and never be so far away. He would not die. Ballantyne was hoarse but he closed his eyes and croaked epithets into the night. "Come and get me, motherfuckers. Come and get me. You assholes. Bastards." Ballantyne opened his eyes to see that the wind and tide had swept him past the burning water and out into the open sea.

Sandhaven had approached to within two hundred feet of Piper Alpha when the MCP-01 riser blew. Captain Sean Ennis was speaking to his Z-boat's coxswain, Ian Letham, who had just snatched some men from one of the legs of the rig. The next second, all Ennis could see was a solid mass of flame covering the boat. The radio sizzled with static. The explosion looked to him like napalm in the movies. The image of the destruction of the beach village in *Apocalypse Now* jumped into his head. The heat was so intense he threw *Sandhaven*'s prop in gear, rang full ahead, and hoped for the best. For twenty minutes, he called his Z-boat, hoping for a reply but knowing that he was not going to get one.

One hundred and seventy-five feet above the sea the inferno was devouring the helideck. Just before the MCP-01 riser blew, Mark Reid had abandoned his refuge next to the refrigerated food container and gone up. He found other men on the helideck, clusters of them jitterbugging in a macabre dance to avoid the flames. When the riser blew, the fire swirled around Reid and all the others as if a devilish entity were toying with them, no longer giving them any way to avoid it. Reid instinctively lifted his hands in front of his face and felt a stinging tingle as his skin vaporized. He dropped his hands and saw shadows of men moving around in the orange darkness, looking down the ladders, turning away from the intense fire, moving to the edge of the landing pad. Near the radio shack, a tongue of flame flared up as though alive with evil intent and one group of men vanished. Right in front of him, Reid watched David Kinrade, the radio operator, run to the edge of the pad and out into the sky. Another man followed him. Reid felt the rubber-impregnated canvas of the landing pad melting. His boots were sticking to its surface. From that moment, conscious decisions became impossible. Reid ran for the edge of the helideck and threw himself into the night. His shirt was on fire. His hands were burned to the bone. He was in the air for six seconds. One. Two. Three. Four. Five. Six. His only thought as he fell was: What have I done?

Reid hit the water in perfect form, feet down, toes pointed, his butt clenched. He was underwater for what seemed like forever until the buoyancy of his life vest shot him to the surface. His left arm was killing him. The vest was twisted so he was awkwardly on his back. He saw other men flying through the air on fire, most of them hitting the water like sacks of sand. In the dirty orange light from the burning rig, another man ten feet away from him struggled with his own life jacket. Reid kicked over to him and helped him with the jacket. He didn't know the man, a bearded fellow who was shivering and talking in unintelligible bursts of pure fright. Reid put his arms around him and muttered the phrase that had always soothed him when his mother said it to him as a little boy.

"There. There. There."

Fifteen

NIGHT

On *Silver Pit,* Ed Punchard made himself look away from the inferno above him and tended to the men coming over the side from the Z-boat. The air was an orange haze filled with chunks of debris that sizzled when they hit the water. Punchard heard the metallic plonks of some of them hitting the wheelhouse above him. The rest of the noise from the incineration of the rig was painful, a jet-turbine roar pierced by the tormented shrieks of fracturing steel. Punchard picked out the hopeful *fut-fut* of a chopper through the hellish din but he never saw it.

Captain John Sabourn kept *Silver Pit* jogging four hundred yards from the rig. After a piece of flaming wreckage hit just below the bridge windows, he hollered down that he couldn't stay where he was for much longer. He had watched the chunk of fire come straight at him and tail down at the last instant to slam into the bulkhead below, all of it happening in a strange kind of slow motion. After it hit, Sabourn thought, God, if I come out of this alive I will never ever be frightened of dying again.

Punchard had scribbled a dozen names on his list of survivors who were aboard *Silver Pit.* Most of them were in pretty good shape with a few cuts and first-degree burns. Now, the Z-boat returned with men so badly wounded that some of them could not climb up the rope net and had to be pulled aboard. Punchard was lightheaded, struggling to keep his vision from blurring. He felt like he had dropped from the sky into a wartime newsreel showing the oil-smeared, blackened faces of men being rescued from the wreck of a battleship. They had exactly the same expressions he had seen in the old films, masks of dull blankness, pain, and horror. Their wounds were terrifying.

Bob Carey managed the net, smiled through his shock, and collapsed on deck. His head was hairless, the back of it burned to the bone which was startlingly white. Erland Grieve came over the rail, soot-black with suppurating pits on his hands and face that hurt him so bad he yelped when Stan McCleod tried to drape a blanket over him. McNeill and his Z-boat crew got a man to the net, but he could do nothing but hang there. Punchard and the others at the rail reached down to help and what they saw made their knees go weak. One of them lurched to the side and vomited. The man on the net was Eric Brianchon, the only Frenchman on Piper Alpha, a thirty-two-year-old electronics tech from the Limousin farm country. Everybody liked him because he always seemed to be amused by whatever was right in front of him. Brianchon clung to the net, delirious and fighting off the men above who were trying to pry his hands off the ropes to haul him up. He was nearly naked, his clothes blown off except for a few strips around his wrists, waist, and ankles. His flesh was a putrid shade of gray-white with patches of stubbly black on his arms and face and curling strips of transparent skin. Brianchon lost consciousness. The men were able to pull him onto the deck where he woke up again and started screaming. Carson rushed over from tending Erland Grieve, instinctively performing triage though he had never before understood what that word and the decisions he was making could mean.

"What about Grieve?" Punchard asked Carson.

"Oh, just a little sunburn," Carson joked. Grieve chuckled, nodded, and took a drag off a cigarette. The faint humor in the moment was a balm. Carson grabbed Punchard's shoulder, looked him in the eyes, and said, "It'll be okay, Ed. Stay with it. Help me."

Stan McCleod took Grieve toward the sick bay. With a deliberate calmness, Carson directed Punchard and Andy Carrol in lifting Brianchon. They slid a stretcher under the Frenchman, who was now sobbing uncontrollably. From the foredeck boarding area, they wrestled their load along the narrow weather deck between the rail and the wheelhouse, turned a corner at the entrance to the canteen, and tilted the stretcher to get it through the narrow hatch. The stretcher banged against the door jamb. Brianchon cried out, more of a whimper than the agonized screams on the net. Punchard couldn't remember Brianchon's first name. Trying to remember it pulled him out of the daze into which he had fallen, quivering and yelling curses at the stupidity of whoever agreed to let an old fishing boat serve as a standby ship in an oil rig emergency.

"Assholes. Assholes," Punchard said. "Motherfucking assholes."

Punchard's anger soothed him. The fury meant nothing as communication but vented an unnamed outrage that had been boiling in him since he'd left the rig. Carson clucked at Punchard and told him to lift as they crossed the watertight threshold and made their way down the tight corridor to the stateroom set aside as a sick bay. Grieve was already there, led under his own power by Stan McCleod to one of the lower bunks. Carson moved Grieve to a chair, then tumbled Brianchon as gently as possible into the berth.

Punchard stood up, passed the stretcher out the door, and looked around. There were no saline drips. Burn victims needed saline drips for hydration. There was nothing, nothing at all that was going to do any good. The cabin was a regular stateroom with linoleum floors, beige walls and ceiling, and the sea-damp aromas of cigarettes and fifty years of sweating men. Punchard was sure that Brianchon, Grieve, and Carey were only the first of many who would need more than a stretcher and a bunk to stay alive. He was muttering obscenities at Occidental and the inequities of life offshore when Carson shook him and said, "Stay here with him, Ed. Sit down." Punchard sat in the other chair in the stateroom. Carson patted him on the shoulder and left.

Punchard looked down at Brianchon and thought, Eric. He remembered that the Frenchman spoke very little English. Once, when they had both been in Barry Barber's office in the dive complex they'd had a disjointed but friendly conversation about Grand Prix racing, Jaguar's recent victory in the Le Mans twenty-four-hour race, and France's great driver Alain Prost.

"Eric," Punchard said to the moaning lump in the berth. "Do you remember we talked in the office about Alain Prost?"

Brianchon stopped moaning and looked directly at Punchard, his eyes focused for the first time since he came aboard *Silver Pit*. Brianchon mumbled, "Alain Prost." Then, as though commanded by his pain, he fell into a hoarse sob that sent his agony into Punchard like a knife. Punchard was only able to take it for a couple of minutes before he left the stateroom, sorry and guilty to be leaving Eric but unable to remain a witness to his suffering. There was nothing he could do, Punchard told himself. He was of more use outside helping with the others.

Back on deck, Punchard's spirits soared when he saw that John Barr and two more divers were alive, wet but unhurt, sitting on the hatch cover wrapped in blankets. Punchard shook hands with them, added their names to his list, and asked if he could do anything for them. One of the divers said he needed a cigarette. Punchard didn't smoke, but walked across the deck to one of the ship's crew who was passing out tea to the survivors. He asked the man where the bond store was, the man told Punchard it was around the corner next to the canteen but that he couldn't get cigarettes because only the captain had a key and he wasn't going to ask him for it because he was bloody fucking busy running the boat.

"Look," Punchard barked, the bile of a few minutes ago at Brianchon's bedside rising anew. "One of the survivors wants a cigarette. Give me an ax, and I'll open the bloody bond."

The tension of the confrontation washed over the men surrounding Punchard and the steward who was backing away from the furious diver. One of the other crewmen stepped between the two, offered Punchard his own cigarettes and a lighter, and it was over. Punchard looked at his list and breathed deeply as he realized how many men from the dive team were still missing.

Five hundred yards away on the other side of Piper Alpha, Keith Cunningham was alive in the water, swimming around the base of one of *Tharos*'s giant legs, shouting to men on deck three stories above him who had no chance of hearing him. A single voice was utterly lost in the roaring fire and the growling of *Tharos*'s water cannons blasting spray over his head. Cunningham had gotten separated from the other divers in the confusion on the spider deck and took his chances in the sea when the Tartan pipeline exploded at 10:22. Still in his diving suit, he swam the five hundred yards to *Tharos* and followed the monstrous vessel as it lumbered toward Piper Alpha. After twenty minutes of treading water and screaming into the orange night, Cunningham found a ladder up one of *Tharos*'s legs. On deck, David Olley threw a blanket over the shivering man who materialized from the shadows of *Tharos*'s drill module. Olley led Cunningham below to the door of the sick bay and left him there. Cunningham walked into the room alone and one of the stewards who was setting up to receive survivors asked him who he was and what he wanted. "I've come from Piper Alpha," Cunningham said, with no sense of urgency in his voice. The steward and two other crewmen in the sick bay finally realized that they had their first survivor onboard. They swarmed Cunningham with attention, most of which he swatted away. "I'm fine," he insisted. "It's going to get worse."

Bill Barron became the second survivor to board *Tharos* a few minutes later. He refused to go below with Barry Goodwin and five other men from the Z-boat, all of them terrified but none of them seriously hurt. Instead, Barron stood on deck, unable to tear his eyes away from the burning rig. Several crewmen approached him, but Barron waved them off, frozen in place by shock and a sense of outrage that was building in him like an electrical current. Did the new kid, he couldn't remember his name, did the new kid on his painting crew get off? Christ, Barron thought. There are only a handful of us here. He looked over the side into a light chop blown up by the firestorm and saw what looked like swimmers but could just be pieces of wreckage drifting in the current. *Tharos*'s Z-boat buzzed through them toward its mothership, heavy with men crouched on its inflatable pontoons with lumps of bodies between them on the deck. Another tremendous ball of flame erupted, shedding daylight over the sea for miles around. Barron saw men on fire clawing the air as they jumped from the upper levels of Piper Alpha, caught himself hoping that each would straighten out his flailing body before he hit the water, and sagged into disappointment when most of them sent up the big splashes of failed divers. The absurdity of his rooting for the falling men as though they were athletes startled him. I should be dead, Barron thought, but he could not look away from the death in front of him. Repeatedly, Olley's crewmen approached Barron and were repelled by his furious energy.

An hour after the first explosion on Piper Alpha, Alastair Letty finally broke through the chaos on the radio and made contact with the coast guard. As captain of *Tharos*, the largest vessel in the area when disaster struck, he had been monitoring and responding to transmissions from the rig, *Silver Pit, Maersk Cutter, Lowland Cavalier, Sandhaven,* and his own helicopter, which was airborne. Letty instinctively moved toward organizing some kind of systematic response. Every ship within ten miles of Piper Alpha had launched Z-boats, one of which had been lost in the fireball at 10:52, leaving at least six in action. Now, the coast guard told Letty that he was officially in charge of the rescue operations. A Nimrod marine patrol aircraft had taken off and would soon be circling overhead at thirty thousand feet to track ships and helicopters on radar. Four Sea King rescue helicopters were on the way, each equipped with a hoist and basket with crewmen trained to jump into the water for survivors or drop to a ship's deck to direct an evacuation. All aircraft would be in radio contact with *Tharos* as the command center. The first chopper was thirty minutes out. Letty's next call was from Occidental headquarters in Aberdeen. This time pulling back from the rig because of the possibility of deadly hydrogen sulfide gas was an order instead of a suggestion. Letty obeyed. He engaged his thrusters and anchor winches to begin moving *Tharos* eight hundred yards further back to set up his command post there. He relayed his own orders to the rest of the rescue flotilla. The supply boat *Loch Shuna,* which had diverted from its shore-bound course, idled on station a mile west of the rig to control the radio traffic among the Z-boats. Making plans and giving orders was an immense relief to Letty. He had been suffering under the worst mariner's curse of all—helplessness—since the first fire erupted from Piper Alpha.

Aboard *Loch Shuna*'s own Z-boat, coxswain Ian Muir idled three hundred feet from Piper Alpha's southeast corner, squinting through the smoke and fire from the last explosion that was consuming the entire rig. He saw men waving at the edge of the decks high above him, some of them on fire. He watched them jump, some of them from low enough down to have a chance of surviving. Most hit the water and were carried back under the rig where the sea was steaming and strewn with burning wreckage. One of Muir's two outboard engines had been cutting out since he left *Loch Shuna*, so he and his crew were leery of making a high-speed pass under the rig from which they might not return if the engines quit. It made no sense to embark on a suicide mission when the goal was to save the men in the water. While Muir debated what to do next, his radio crackled with a transmission from the *Maersk Cutter*. There were survivors spotted in the water away from the rig, drifting to the northwest. Muir nudged his throttles forward, felt the satisfying thrust of both engines, and moved slowly through a maze of wood, fiberglass paneling, and tangled metal. Two hundred feet from the rig, the heat was so intense they couldn't look at it without covering their faces with their arms. Muir shouted, "There," and pointed to an orange hump in the oil-thick surface to starboard. It wasn't moving. As Muir turned his boat toward the bobbing shape, he heard a hoarse cry from open water away from the rig. Go to the living, he thought, and turned toward the voice in the darkness. There were two of them. One looked unconscious. The other was awake, peering up into Muir's flashlight beam with alert bright eyes in a blackened face.

Mark Reid had been in the water for forty-five minutes since surviving his desperate jump from the helideck 175 feet above the sea. He talked to God while he waited, made a deal that if he could see his wife, Mary, and his thirteen-week-old son, Marc, just one more time he would agree to die. Reid had no idea how that was going to happen, but he made the bargain anyway. He wanted to see the Clyde River, too. Glasgow. Simple things. He imagined all of it, carefully arranging the pictures as they flowed into his mind. Reid hurt all over. His right arm was dead weight, blessedly numb. It frightened him. He hated the thought of being a one-armed man. The rest of his body stung from the seawater, his face especially when the oil-stinking water splashed over him. Reid had held on to the bearded man until his own survival suit got waterlogged and he had to fight to keep himself afloat. The other man, who stopped moving in a few minutes, drifted a few feet away from him on the current taking both of them away from the burning rig. When the fire above him blossomed into a thunderhead, Reid forced himself to submerge to get out of the heat. When the flames subsided, Reid heard the Z-boats whining in the darkness around him, but none came near until long after he had given up hope.

Ian Muir and his crew had trouble pulling Reid into their boat because he and his suit full of water weighed three hundred pounds. All of them had retrieved men from the sea in drills, but then there was no fire, no smoke, and no terror. With Reid aboard, Muir went to the silent man near him. He was breathing but unconscious, his head flopping unnaturally around the padded ring of his life vest. Knowing that a man with a broken neck might die if they moved him, Muir and his men had no choice but to pull the bearded man into the Z-boat. A minute later, they found two others with the same kind of injuries, all of them near death. They went back toward the rig, guarded by the spray from the *Maersk Cutter*'s water cannons. The first man O'Neill had seen and turned away from to rescue the screaming Reid from the darkness was still there, still not moving. When they got him alongside, his arms hung limply in the water and his head flopped obscenely when they moved him. There was no question that he was dead.

Bob Ballantyne, too, had been in the water for forty-five minutes since he'd jumped from Piper Alpha. The explosion that broke his grip on the leg of the rig to which he clung after jumping twenty feet into the sea set him free to drift with the northerly current. The fall hadn't hurt him at all. For a while, the only pain he felt was a soreness in his wrists where his survival suit had melted and the stinging on his face. Ballantyne screamed until he forgot that he was screaming, an angry rant at Piper Alpha, the universe, the goddamned oil that had forever fucked up the beautiful stretch of the Scottish coast where his precious Highlands met the North Sea. He cursed the North Sea. He wished he were more badly injured so he couldn't think about what was happening to him. He had survived the fire. Now he was going to die alone in the ocean. His suit was full of water. He had lost feeling in his legs. Maybe he was badly injured. Maybe his back was broken. He closed his eyes. When the lights of the *Lowland Cavalier* winked over his shoulder, he thought he was hallucinating. He noticed that he was still screaming. From above, a rope with a big knot on the end of it splashed into the water next to him. Ballantyne grabbed it but that was all he could do. He couldn't pull himself up. Men on the ship above were shouting at him in what sounded like Norwegian. He tried again, but failed to get high enough out of the water to grab the tangle net on the side of the hull. "Fuck it," Ballantyne yelled. "I'm just going to let this rope go. I can't take it. I'm just going to drift out to sea. I don't care." A voice broke through his desperation. One of the men on the ship was yelling and miming tying a rope around his waist. Ballantyne obeyed. A minute later, three seamen had hauled him on deck where he lay motionless while the water drained from his survival suit. *Lowland Cavalier* had already picked up a dozen drifting men, so their medical supplies had run out. The only thing they could offer him for his burning face was a bag of frozen peas. As Ballantyne lay in a berth belowdecks, he felt the ship shudder under him when another blast shocked the air around Piper Alpha. He banished thoughts of being shipwrecked again and concentrated on the peas on his face. Their cool nubbles were such sublime relief that Ballantyne hoped they would never melt.

On Claymore, twenty-two miles from Piper Alpha, OIM S. B. Sandlin had seen the orange glow on the horizon when the Tartan riser exploded at 10:22 and watched in horror at what looked like a nuclear explosion blossom into the atmosphere when the MCP-01 riser blew a half hour later. Still, Sandlin did not make the decision to turn off the gas and oil pipelines flowing from his rig through Piper Alpha on his own. Just after 11 p.m., his radio crackled with the permission to shut down Claymore. Sticking with the instructions in his procedure manual, Sandlin ordered a staged shutdown, which took a half hour to complete. An emergency shutdown would have stopped everything flowing from Claymore in two minutes, but it would have caused millions of dollars of damage to pumps, valves, and electronic controls. The gas continued to flow to Piper Alpha.

At 11:20, the valve head on the Claymore gas pipeline that passed through Piper Alpha vaporized and exploded. The twenty-two miles of sixteen-inch pipe contained ten million cubic feet of pressurized gas, enough to heat the entire city of Aberdeen for a month. It was the most violent explosion of the four that night, igniting the sky with a bright white disk before settling back into an orange, yellow, and black fireball five times what it had been seconds earlier.

On *Silver Pit*, Ed Punchard and Stan McCleod had organized the rescued divers at the rails to look for survivors. Captain Sabourn had risked coming nearer to Piper Alpha, knowing that minutes were now priceless to men in the water. The rig's fire illuminated the sea so they could clearly see a floating junkyard of hard hats, hunks of wallboard, ceilings, tables, chairs, cartons of canteen supplies, and paper everywhere. There were a startling number of lumps of orange and red survival suits and life vests, some of them moving, some of them still. Punchard could see only one Z-boat anywhere near the wreckage between *Silver Pit* and Piper Alpha, but several others in the distance around the rig. Andy Carrol couldn't stand the sight of so many men in the water and so few of them getting picked up. After watching several orange lumps drift out of view on the current, Carrol left the rail and ran over to Punchard. "Ed. It's insane to have survived the fire and then be lost in the sea," he begged. "Talk to the skipper about getting some more boats over here."

Punchard went up to the bridge. Sabourn was preoccupied with a serious drop in oil pressure that threatened his engines and waved him away. Punchard grabbed the radio mike off the wall himself.

"This is *Silver Pit. Silver Pit.* Calling all ships in the vicinity. There are survivors floating on the surface between *Silver Pit* and *Tharos.* That is between the northwest area and the southwest area of the platform. Any ships with Zodiacs, lifeboats, or small craft of any kind, launch them and come to this area. There are many survivors in the water."

In *Silver Pit*'s Z-boat, the faces of Jimmy McNeill and his crew were burned bright red from the heat. Inside their survival suits, they were soaking wet with sweat. In an hour and a half, they had saved twenty-five men, most of them from ladders leading down the legs of the rig in the heart of the fire but some like a deus ex machina, plucking them from helplessness and certain death in the sea. McNeill happened to be looking up when a man plunged from the helideck, saw the splash where he landed, and pulled him from the water the moment he surfaced. The man was alive for a while, but dead before they got him to *Silver Pit.* They picked up one survivor whose only stitch of clothing was the waistband of his underpants. When they hauled him aboard, the skin of his arm sloughed off and dangled down like a glove. Haffey swallowed the bile that rose in his throat and slapped the horribly burned man to keep him awake while McNeill hollered, "Slap his face. Slap his face. Don't let him flake out." Haffey pulled another man from the sea after watching him sink, rise, sink, rise, and sink again, grabbing him by his hair from underwater and hauling him aboard. After the second fireball, as McNeill steered back under the rig, dodging debris at full speed, Haffey had shouted, "I hope God is looking after us tonight, Jimmy." McNeill yelled back, "Two good men are looking after you tonight, Charlie. Him and me."

When the Claymore riser blew, even McNeill couldn't save his Z-boat. The explosions had devastated Piper Alpha and torn burning holes in the air above the rig, but had also destroyed the oddly delicate balances that kept miles of pipe organized beneath the surface and on the floor of the sea. With three survivors aboard, including the man Haffey had pulled out by the hair, they were about a hundred yards from the rig running for *Silver Pit* when what felt like an earthquake shook the boat. McNeill had no idea what was happening, but he throttled back and yelled to his crew to throw themselves over the wounded men lying on the deck. An instant later the whole boat was airborne, thousands of pounds of engines, wood, rubber, and men, tossed up as though it were a feather in an updraft. Four hundred feet beneath them, a feeder line had ruptured, sending an incendiary gas bubble to the surface that lifted the Z-boat up, held it in the air for a split second, and dropped it ten feet back into the sea. The blast split the bottom of the boat beneath McNeill's feet, sending a column of burning gas past him, singeing off his eyebrows and charring the bags under his eyes as though he had had hot sand thrown in his face.

Incredibly, the engine was still running, but McNeill's Z-boat was mortally injured. In a minute, water was pooling around his ankles. They were sixty feet from the Piper Alpha, which was now slouching unnaturally to the side with enormous pieces of the rig splashing into the sea around them. McNeill yelled something and pointed toward two men in the water a hundred feet away. Haffey shot his coxswain a look that said, "Suicide."

"Well, are we going to go for them," McNeill yelled over the roar above them.

Haffey, Kiloh, and one of the survivors on the floor yelled in one voice, "Go, go, go, go."

Seconds later, Ian Fowler and Harry Calder, who had dropped into the sea when the floor of the pipe deck collapsed, were lying on the floor of the boat with the other three survivors. They were blackened with soot, dazed but conscious. On the way back to *Silver Pit,* McNeill's engine sputtered and died. The boat settled and flooded. The crew that had saved the lives of thirty men waited with their last survivors to be rescued themselves. The wreck of the Z-boat was still buoyant with air in its hull chambers, the sea was warm, and they could hear more boats buzzing nearby. The crew and the men they rescued were in the water but safe. *Silver Pit* was less than a hundred yards away. O'Neill floated on his back, easy with himself as the adrenaline bled from his system, knowing that he and his men had done what they had to do that night.

Five minutes after O'Neill, his crew, and five survivors went into the water, the Z-boat from *Maersk Cutter* picked them up and took them to *Silver Pit*. Following maritime protocol, McNeill was the last man off his boat. As McNeill hung on the boarding net, he heard a sound behind him that reminded him of those films of razing old buildings with carefully placed charges of dynamite. The noise was first a series of sharp reports like gunshots, louder than the fire or anything he had heard that night, followed by a horrendous creaking. He looked over his shoulder and watched the slouching oil rig dismantle itself into rubble.

Above McNeill on *Silver Pit*'s deck, Punchard, McCleod, and the other divers stopped what they were doing and watched an escalation of what all of them, until that moment, believed was the worst thing they had ever witnessed. Now, the iconic pyramid of the drilling derrick pirouetted from its base and plunged needle-tip downward as though intending to pierce the heart of the sea. One crane followed, then the other. A massive cascade of steel plummeted through the internal framework of the jacket, tearing beams and struts from the legs as it fell and triggering a tsunami that washed all the Z-boats away from the rig and into the surrounding darkness. For a few seconds, Piper Alpha paused in its death throes. Then, with terrible punctuation to all that had gone before, the accommodation module separated from the remaining steel frames and hurtled 150 feet down into the sea. The gigantic rectangular steel box trailed smoke and fire that continued to burn even after it hit the water, sending out waves that dwarfed those of the collapse of moments ago. For an agonizing minute, O'Neill, Punchard, McCleod, Sabourn, Bill Barron still at the rail on *Tharos*'s deck, and every other man with a view of what had happened were frozen in contemplation of how best to reach the men in the floating accommodation module. There were at least eighty of them in there, maybe a hundred, maybe more. Many of the survivors on *Silver Pit* and the other ships had begun their fight for their own lives in the galley that was now part of the wreckage in the water. Then, in a seething eruption of steaming water and with a gurgling snort, the surface of the sea split apart and the accommodation module disappeared. On the ships, the witnesses froze. Finally, the sound of helicopters in the air around them broke through the horror of what they had just seen. There wasn't much left of Piper Alpha. The biggest piece was the jagged wreckage of the drilling floor, which had once been part of the production deck. From it, the tops of the pipelines and wells burned furiously, sending their roaring, gas-fed flames hundreds of feet into the sky.

Sixteen

THAROS

The first of the coast guard Sea King helicopters landed on *Tharos* five minutes later. *Maersk Logger,* another of the Norwegian supply boats that had responded to Piper Alpha's Maydays, was alongside unloading survivors that had been delivered to her by the Z-boats. A four-foot swell had risen as the night deepened and the continental convections surrounding the North Sea encouraged a steady light wind. The only way to get survivors onto *Tharos* from a smaller boat bobbing below was one man at a time in a rope basket slung under a crane. The men coming from *Maersk Logger* and the nine already aboard *Tharos* did not have life-threatening injuries. Medic David Olley told Captain Letty that he could use the first two or three choppers to evacuate thirty of the men who had been working aboard *Tharos* but who had nothing to do during rescue operations. Getting them off the ship would free space for what Letty and Olley assumed would be more than a hundred survivors. Their expectations crashed when Piper Alpha collapsed. Letty was beset by the horrible possibility that the survivors he had on board, with those already on *Silver Pit,* might be all there were going to be. He fought off pangs of regret that *Tharos* had never gotten close enough to save anyone with its gangway, gathered his strength, and ordered his water cannons shut down to make it easier for landing the helicopters. There was no point pouring water into Piper Alpha, which was now only blackened slag draped over three legs.

The second wave of two rescue choppers landed on *Tharos* just before midnight with five doctors from Aberdeen. After Dr. Graham Page at the Aberdeen Royal Infirmary saw the ITV newscast about a fire offshore the night before, one of his first phone calls to alert the city's emergency forces had been to Dr. Ronnie Strachan. Strachan was the head of a group of doctors specializing in burns, trauma, and other workplace accidents. David Olley was happy to hand over his sick bay to the doctors, who confirmed his evaluation that none of the nine survivors already aboard *Tharos* were in danger of losing their lives. The doctors checked the saline drips and unloaded hard-shell boxes of their own pain medication, burn ointment, electrolytes, sutures, splints, scalpels, and anesthesia. Then they sat down, accepted cups of tea from one of Olley's stewards, and waited.

On *Silver Pit,* the engine oil line finally blew just after Letty broadcast a call for all vessels to bring survivors to *Tharos*. George Carson was the only man who could fix it, so he had to leave the survivors in his sick bay in the care of the divers, including the badly injured Eric Brianchon, Erland Grieve, and Bob Carey. Carson knew that unless *Silver Pit* could get those three men to *Tharos,* or a helicopter could winch them up from the stern, none of them would live much longer. What he saw in the engine room sickened him. One of the main oil feed hoses had ruptured when the explosions on Piper Alpha tossed the old fishing boat around. Another hose connection had pulled free of its fitting, leaving stripped threads to which it was going to be almost impossible to attach a replacement. When his engine died, Sabourn instantly checked the angle of his drift on the current. Mercifully, it looked like it was going to take him past Piper Alpha with at least a hundred yards of clearance. Without power, he was broadside to the swell and rolling heavily, which was going to make it harder for the choppers to lift injured men from a pitching deck.

When the awful silence of a ship without an engine startled Punchard and McCleod, they huddled and decided what to do when a helicopter arrived. They heard the choppers landing on *Tharos* and figured it was only a matter of minutes before they could call in one of the Sea Kings to hoist Brianchon, Carey, and Grieve, along with six others with bad burns, cuts, and broken bones. Punchard and McCleod went up to the bridge, where Sabourn told them that the back of the boat was the only safe place from which to winch men up into the helicopter. The injured survivors had to be carried by stretcher from the center deck or the sick bay to the stern. Punchard went down to the canteen where divers Tony Payne and Chris Niven volunteered to carry the men along the narrow weather deck, which was slick with hydraulic fluid from a leaking davit. Carson popped up out of the engine room hatch with the bad news that he was hours away from getting the engine started, then disappeared again.

While McLeod, Payne, and Niven strapped Brianchon and Carey to the stretchers, Punchard went to the bridge. The radio was crackling with a call from a helicopter. He told the pilot there were thirty-five survivors aboard. Nine were seriously injured but three so badly that they had to get off right now. The pilot calmly said, "Two minutes."

On the stern, *Silver Pit*'s new paint job included a bright yellow circle as a target for lowering the basket from a hovering helicopter. There was room only for Punchard to direct the chopper, the stretcher bearers, and the injured man. The chopper approached upwind, with the burning remains of Piper Alpha behind it, hovering thirty feet over the deck. Punchard waved an okay, Payne and Niven wrestled Brianchon's stretcher into position, and the winch man descended from the chopper in an orange fiberglass basket the shape of a coffin. *Silver Pit* snapped through a particularly violent arc of its roll, slamming the winch man against the rail before he was able to jump to the deck.

In seconds, they moved the moaning Brianchon from the stretcher to the basket. They got Carey and Grieve off before the pilot radioed down to the winch man that he couldn't hold any more wounded. He had already picked up survivors from *Lowland Cavalier*. He would be back. As Punchard waved the helicopter away, he was stunned to see a man leaning from the rescue hatch pointing a television camera at him.

Paul Berriff and his sound man from Grampian Television in Aberdeen had been exhilarated two hours earlier when the rescue helicopter on which they were filming a documentary happened upon Piper Alpha just as the first fire roared into the night sky. Their luck at actually witnessing a major offshore accident was incredible, a once-in-a-lifetime opportunity to capture a catastrophe on film. By the time Berriff leaned out the hatch over *Silver Pit* to film Ed Punchard waving and the stern shrinking dramatically as the chopper lifted up, he and his crew were nauseous and stricken dumb by what they had seen and photographed. Documentarians feast on real moments of drama that punch through the hours and hours of humdrum events they encounter most of the time, but the holocaust on Piper Alpha and the sight of men on fire falling into the sea destroyed their enthusiasm for their luck. Berriff decided to go back to *Tharos,* try to interview survivors there, and get his film to Aberdeen in time for the morning news.

The first whisker of dawn brightened the eastern sky at 3:45 a.m., throwing a faint gray light into the sky and silhouetting the still burning snouts of Piper Alpha's gas pipeline risers and wellheads on what was left of the drilling floor. One flare boom remained on a corner of the wreckage, drooping toward the sea like a contorted, broken limb. George Carson got *Silver Pit*'s engine running at 4 a.m. A half hour later, Sabourn eased his tattered, singed little trawler alongside *Tharos* and unloaded the rest of the thirty-seven men he and his crew had rescued. There were twenty-five other survivors already aboard *Tharos.* Sixty-two in all. The ships, Z-boats, and helicopters searched for more but brought back only charred and mangled bodies. Captain Letty ordered a morgue set up in the helicopter hangar. A steady stream of Sea Kings and Sikorskys landed and took off with the living, then with the dead. Bill Barron was on the very first of them because he had no visible injuries at all and he was able to hold the IV bottle dripping saline and painkiller into Eric Brianchon's arm.

The sun rose at 4:37.

Seventeen

THE MORNING NEWS

The first helicopter landed at the Aberdeen Royal Infirmary at dawn after an hour-and-ten-minute flight from *Tharos*. Bill Barron spent the trip on his knees, holding an IV pouch over Eric Brianchon, who lurched every few minutes as though waking from a bad dream. Barron soothed him until he sagged back into a Demerol haze and lay quietly on the floor, charred and shivering but alive, a sight so terrifying to Barron that he had to squint to look at him. There were five other men sprawled in the Sea King's passenger cabin—Erland Grieve, Bob Carey, Ian Fowler, Harry Calder, and Mark Reid—all of them with bandages over their burns. Being alive, in a helicopter, on the way to a real hospital, was the most priceless gift imaginable. They sat quietly propped against the cabin walls, in pain, but grateful.

Barron had made the flight between Piper Alpha and Aberdeen many times, but this was his first landing at the hospital instead of the airport at Dyce. When the engines relaxed and the chopper began its descent, Barron leaned over Brianchon to look out the window. He was relieved to see that they were no longer over open ocean. It was still too dark to pick out his house, but he saw the faint shimmer of the River Don pass beneath him, then the still flickering spangles of street lamps meandering among the buildings downtown. Over the outskirts of the west end, as the sheen of the water in the Rubislaw granite quarry winked up at him, the nose of the helicopter pitched up on its final approach. The Sea King hovered and settled into a circle of lights on the ground with a bright yellow H at its center. Hospital, Barron thought. Helipad. Home.

He hadn't slept in twenty-four hours. His thoughts did not seem to flow from his own head, but from someplace beyond his control. All he could do was listen and sometimes speak them to remind himself that he was alive. "I wonder if the fish from the tanks in the galley escaped into the water." "I have to call Trish right away."

Graham Page had the hospital ready for two hundred survivors. After the first mention of a disaster offshore on the ITV news at 10:30 the night before, he had spent an hour on the phone summoning doctors, nurses, and Archie Robb's social workers. He dispatched the doctors to *Tharos*. Grampian Television and ITV news readers were back on the air at 11:30 p.m., looking grim and tired. They wouldn't have film of what was happening offshore until morning, but over stock photographs of Piper Alpha, they confirmed their sketchy reports of an explosion and fire. They promised bulletins through the night. In the hour since the story broke, what they had earlier described as an accident had assumed the dimensions of a catastrophe. At 12:30 a.m., all stations broadcast the news that Piper Alpha had collapsed into the sea. There were survivors. They would be brought directly to the hospital by helicopter. Immediately, Page's emergency room switchboard lit up with calls. He told his operators to be brief, explain that there were no names yet, and move along to the next call. The queue was endless. Fifteen minutes after the 12:30 news bulletins, the first of hundreds of wives, girlfriends, brothers, sisters, mothers, fathers, and children of men working offshore drove into the hospital parking lot. Most of them were not sure if their man was even working on Piper Alpha. Those who did know were on the edge of panic.

An hour later, forty people had gathered in one of the hospital's waiting rooms, most of them women from Aberdeen, some of them towing sleepy, bewildered children. More arrived in a steady stream, some of them from as far away as Peterhead an hour to the north and Dundee an hour south. Page told the hospital's publicity director, Alan Reid, to move the crowd to the chapel, which could hold a hundred people. Reid gave off the scent of a man forcing himself to remain calm. He was afraid of what the helicopters were going to bring and afraid of the heartbreak he was going to witness. A Church of Scotland minister arrived and took charge of consolation. In the absence of any hard information, the comfort of a word or a touch was all he could offer.

Reid set up a whiteboard in the front of the room and wrote the estimated time of arrival of the first helicopter: 0330. A little more than an hour away. Hospital kitchen workers brought in a table on which they arranged cups, urns of tea and coffee, and plates of shortbread and plain biscuits. The people in the chapel and a waiting room next door that was absorbing the overflow didn't eat or drink much. By 2 a.m., there were more than two hundred of them, most clustered into little groups built around family ties, friendships, and the contractors for whom their men worked. There were women and children whose men worked for Occidental, but no one from the Aberdeen office had come to the hospital. With an hour to go before the first chopper arrived, word filtered in that Piper Alpha had collapsed into the sea and what was left standing was still on fire. There were still no names of survivors. A woman in the waiting room lost control and began screaming, "Those bastards at Oxy have killed my husband. Those bastards have killed my husband."

At Occidental headquarters, a twenty-minute drive from the hospital, Kate Graham and the rest of the Oxy staff knew that many men were dead or missing. They did not know their names. The single satellite line to *Tharos* was jammed with traffic from ships, planes, and helicopters, so very little about survivors was getting through. Early on, when the first reports of explosions and fire trickled in, the Oxy men and women who had reported to work in the middle of the night had been devastated by the possibility that two or three men were likely to have died. Around midnight, a transmission from the Nimrod airplane over the scene described Piper Alpha's collapse. A few minutes later, a man from the radio room had walked into the press office, propped a whiteboard on an easel, and wrote: 190 MISSING.

That can't be, Graham thought, leaning against a desk to keep from sagging to the floor. There must be some boats around with the other men onboard. It can't be as many as that. She told her three assistants to hold off giving any numbers to the clutch of television and newspaper reporters in Oxy's lobby.

At the hospital, Page and Reid tried to manage the media arriving now from as far away as Edinburgh and Glasgow by appearing every few minutes to tell them that nothing had changed. The first chopper was still due at 0330. By then they'd know more. Page spent most of his time tending to the hysteria that was about to turn three hundred people into a mob. They had now spilled out of the waiting room and the chapel and crowded around the road leading to the emergency room door. Like most physicians, Page was no stranger to violence, death, and heartbreak, but these women, who did not know whether their men were dead or alive, were the most wretched he had ever encountered. Reid could only tell them that there were survivors. He did not know how many. He did not know their names.

The crowd surged from the classroom and the chapel at the first faint whapping of helicopter rotors, a sound that had become as familiar as birdsong on the coast of the North Sea. They lined the hundred-yard asphalt driveway between the emergency room entrance and the landing pad as the helicopter roared overhead. The big yellow Sea King settled on the helipad, its landing lights glaring against the still dark sky, its wind forcing everyone beneath it to tuck their eyes under crooked arms. For an eternity, no one moved until the turbines wound down and the blades slowed. From four ambulances, their backs toward the landing pad, stretcher bearers shuffled toward the chopper door as it slid open, instinctively ducking their heads though the still turning rotor was well above them. Brianchon was first off, with Barron reaching to his full height to keep the IV bag elevated as the ambulance medics pulled the unconscious man onto a gurney. Another medic looked Barron square in the eyes, took the bag away, and walked him toward one of the ambulances.

"There's nothing wrong with me," Barron said.

"We'll check you over anyway."

"I want to call my wife."

"Soon."

At the door to the hospital, the crowd was deathly silent as each ambulance pulled up. Barron walked past them under his own power with a medic holding his arm. He averted his eyes from the blurry wash of faces all desperately hoping for word of loved ones.

Ten minutes later, Barron sat on a couch in the emergency room lobby and dialed his home number on the telephone somebody handed him. He looked out the door and watched the Sea King lift off the pad and turn east for the sea. Seconds later, another helicopter whined into view to replace it, nose-high, howling. The crowd surged against the road in the glare of the streetlights. After many rings, Barron heard the miraculous, sleep-addled voice of his wife.

"Barron residence."

"Trish, I'm okay."

"Of course you are, Willie, but why are you calling in the middle of the night."

"Piper Alpha blew up. I'm okay. Nothing at all wrong with me."

"My God, Willie. My God. Was anybody hurt?"

"Come pick me up, Trish. Just come right now and pick me up. I'm at the hospital."

The second chopper arrived with seven badly burned men. They filled every gurney and bed in the emergency room and lent a tone of wartime urgency to what had been a carefully made plan. The medics bringing the men from the chopper performed triage, sorting the few with life-threatening wounds from those who could wait for treatment. A doctor took Barron down a corridor into an examining room where he looked him over again, this time more carefully. He didn't have a scratch on him. The doctor patted Barron like he would a child with a skinned knee, and settled him on a couch in the waiting room. Two more helicopters had landed with more survivors. Everyone was calm, but the ER was now crowded and bristling with tension about how many more were coming. Nobody noticed Trish Barron rush through the emergency room door to her husband who stood, opened his arms as though to say, "Look. I'm just fine," then draped them around her. Without a word to anyone, the Barrons walked out, drove to their cottage on the north side of town by the River Don, and put on the tea kettle. Ten minutes later, the blue flashing lights of a police car washed the dawn light from their front window. Holding his hat, a policeman told Barron that he was sorry but he had to take him to the Skean Dhu Hotel at Dyce airport. All survivors were being debriefed there. It was orders from Occidental and the chief of police. "Do I have a choice?" Barron asked. The policeman told him he didn't.

Ed Punchard came ashore with six other men on the ninth helicopter just after seven in the morning. The badly burned and injured were already at the hospital, so the ride wasn't a lot different from an ordinary commute from the rig except for the astonishing number of ships he saw steaming toward what was left of Piper Alpha. As the chopper made landfall, the lush summer-green coastline over-whelmed him with its beauty. Punchard began to cry, ducked his face to hide, then noticed other men crying, too. After the accom-modation module went into the sea, the Z-boats brought only bodies to *Tharos*, some of them charred so badly they were barely recognizable as human beings, others pristine and naked as though emerging from a bath. The divers who had been living on *Tharos* to work on the Chanter pipeline had been pressed into service to handle the corpses. The dead waited until the sixty-two survivors had gone to shore. There were only fifteen bodies from Piper Alpha, two from *Sandhaven*'s Z-boat. Everybody else was still missing: 150 men. The ships, choppers, and Z-boats were still picking their way around the flaming wreckage and rafts of debris in the water but finding no one alive and very few of the dead.

Punchard stepped from the helicopter into a ring of ambulances surrounded by thirty or forty reporters and cameramen, lights aglare, boom mikes thrust at whomever would tolerate them. Punchard blinked them away, savoring for a moment the damp aroma of morning soil. Everyone from his chopper was able to walk. The medics showed them into two of the ambulances, which moved at a sedate pace up the road to the emergency room door. The crowd surrounding the driveway watched them unload with such fierce longing in their eyes that Punchard recoiled from their anguish. Some held their hands out, imploring acknowledgment like people at a parade groping a famous politician. Many shouted names of men Punchard knew and men he did not know. Someone yelled, "How many more? How many more?"

Inside, a nurse put a wrist band on him and led him to an examination room. Punchard asked if there were many survivors. She said nowhere near as many as they were expecting. Punchard said he wanted a telephone. After we're sure you're okay, the nurse said. For ten minutes, a doctor looked him over, checked the foot he had twisted trying to get his boot off when *Silver Pit* towed him through the water. Punchard's sock was bloody, but the doctor couldn't find a cut. She asked if he had breathed in any water or smoke. He shook his head. "You're okay," the doctor said. "Lucky man. Go and get a cup of tea. You can use the telephone now. There's one in the office next door."

Vicky told him she had heard the news that Piper Alpha had blown up. She'd tried calling Occidental on the ordinary line instead of the emergency number given on the television. She was passed from the operator to a man who told her that Edwin Punchard was on the list of survivors. Vicky said she was fine until it hit her that if the man said there was a list of survivors there must be a list of men who were dead, at which point she started crying. Her husband was alive, but she had no way to know how badly injured he was until she got his call from the Aberdeen hospital three hours later. She cried again on the phone. Punchard told her he would be in Cornwall that night.

The last of ten helicopters with survivors landed just after seven. Stan McCleod was among the five aboard, none of whom was hurt badly enough to be carried. The crowd around the landing pad and the road to the emergency room had swelled to more than five hundred, including the reporters and camera crews. At 7:30 a.m., Alan Reid told them that a massive fleet of ships, planes, and helicopters was still searching the waters around Piper Alpha, but for the time being, no more helicopters were on the way to the hospital. After the announcement nobody moved. Five minutes later, a rumor circulated among the stunned wives, girlfriends, children, parents, and friends of Piper Alpha's men that a shipload of survivors was at that moment headed for the Aberdeen docks. To add dimension to this false hope, someone embroidered the rumor with the fact that the crew of the ship were Russians. Reid heard the rumor about the Russian ship. He immediately stood in front of the crowd and said there was no truth to it.

By four in the morning, there were still doubts about numbers and names at Oxy headquarters. Kate Graham told an Aberdeen *Press and Journal* reporter that only 39 survivors had been positively identified by rescuers; 193 dead or missing. The newspaper published a special 5 a.m. edition with its largest headline in its history. 193 OILMEN FEARED DEAD. News anchors read the same numbers in television news bulletins at 6, 6:30, and 7 a.m., over some of the footage from the camera crew that had been aboard the rescue helicopter.

In Nairn, on the north coast, Yvonne Gillanders tapped on her mother's bedroom door, opened it a crack, and asked, "Mom. What rig is dad on?" "Why, the Piper, honey. Same as before. Why do you ask?" Yvonne told her that the news the night before and just now said there had been a terrible explosion and men had been killed. Ann Gillanders rose, went to her kitchen, and dialed the number of her husband Ian's contractor in Aberdeen, the Wood Group. The line rang and rang. She tried Occidental. Wood. Occidental. For two hours. Finally, a woman at the Wood Group picked up the phone. "Is Ian Gillanders alive?" "I'm sorry," the woman said. "I've checked the list of survivors and Ian is not on it. I'm sorry." Soon, a policeman came to Gillanders's home, now filled with friends and relatives. Ann wouldn't go to the door. From the parlor, she heard the words "missing, presumed dead." Ann said, "Missing?" loudly enough for the policeman to hear her through the gasp of her sob. He took a step in toward the parlor, looked at her, and said, "You realize that there is not really any hope?" Ann said, "Yes."

In Aberdeen, Bob Ballantyne's girlfriend, Pat Slater, woke at 6:30 to the blaring nuisance of the downstairs doorbell to their third-floor apartment. She and Bob were ordinary working people, departing that reality once in a while with joy and bliss, very grateful to have found each other in midlife after romance had abandoned each of them more than once. Through the tinny speaker of the entryway intercom, a man who said he was a policeman asked if Robert Ballantyne lived there. Her first thought was, What has he done now? Ballantyne was an electrician with a poet's soul. He fought authority every chance he got. Pat figured Bob had either been fired, arrested, or worse. She let the policeman in. At her door, he told her that there had been an accident on Piper Alpha. Ballantyne was alive, one of the lucky ones. He was at the hospital asking for Pat. Fifteen minutes later, she was in the car with her sister Anne, who was a psychiatric nurse. "Get him talking," Anne said as she drove. "When he finishes talking, get him talking some more." The hospital was chaotic. No one could tell them where to find Ballantyne. They roamed corridors until they blundered into the chapel packed with people sobbing through one of Alan Swinton's many prayers that he began reciting when the last helicopter landed. Pat and Anne ducked out as fast as they could before the agony of the loved ones of lost men rubbed off on them. After more long minutes of looking, they found Ballantyne sitting in a chair in an examination room wearing his orange work coveralls, still black with the oil in which he had drifted for more than an hour. He had given in to anger as he waited for Pat, bitterness toward Occidental, toward the oil business in general, toward the bad luck that put him on Piper Alpha the night before. When he saw her, he gave it all up for relief and made a joke. "I'm terribly sorry, sweetheart," Ballantyne said. "I've lost those new shoes you bought me for our trip to France."

In Glasgow, Mary Reid got a phone call from somebody who said she was a nurse at the Aberdeen hospital. There had been an accident on Piper Alpha, but Mary's husband was alive. He had burns on his arms and face. He couldn't talk right then, but would not calm down until somebody called his wife. Mary hung up the phone, bundled Marc in his bedding, took him to her mother's house, and started the three-and-a-half-hour drive to Aberdeen.

Marlene Bremner in Aberdeen awoke to a call from her father, who hadn't slept well in years and watched television at all hours. He said her husband Sandy's oil rig was on fire, that men were being evacuated to the Royal Infirmary. Marlene joined the crowd at the hospital just as Sandy, wrapped in a blanket, walked wide-eyed from a helicopter that had just landed. The medics had to pry them apart when they took Sandy to an examining room.

Grace Whitely got up that morning with a list of things to finish before she and her husband Bob started out that afternoon on a road trip with their caravan club. Bob had been a roustabout on Piper Alpha for four and a half years. They lived for their time together when he was off the rig. Grace saw the news on the television and spent the next two hours dialing the telephone before she was told that Bob was not on the list of survivors.

Janet Heggie refused to believe the voice on the other end of the phone line telling her that her husband, Jimmy, was missing and probably dead. He had left just the afternoon before, and she wasn't sure he had even gotten out to the rig. She hung up and dialed the number for Bawden Drilling for an hour before a woman answered and told her the same thing as the first caller. She went to the hospital anyway.

Margaret Scorgie woke to what she was looking forward to as a day of planning for her daughter Michelle's first birthday. Her husband, Mike, was getting off the rig early to be home for the party. She flicked on the television, saw the images of an oil rig burning in the night, and spent her next hour dialing the number for Bawden Drilling.

Hazel Duncan's husband, Eric, had left Peterhead the morning before, planning to fly to Piper Alpha that evening to begin his two-week shift. If he was aboard the burning rig on the television he would have only been there for an hour or so. Until the social worker rang her bell, Hazel had been able to cling to the possibility that Eric had not gotten there at all.

Elizabeth Boyle went to the hospital after the morning news to look for her fiancé, Bill McGregor. She was sure he could not have died. They were planning to be married in nine weeks.

When the policeman came to Roslyn Duncan's door, she told him she was quite sure that her husband, John, was on Tartan, not Piper Alpha. The man looked at his shoes, looked back at her, and said, "No. He was on Piper Alpha." Roslyn argued with him for five minutes before giving in to the horror of what the man was telling her.

Margaret Sutton knew the moment she answered her door at an odd hour in midmorning that her husband, Terry, was dead. She just knew.

Karen Munro, pregnant with her second child with one still in diapers, saw the morning news, went to the hospital, waited for three hours, and went home. An hour later, a policeman came to her door. In shock, she said, "I think Bruce would have been asleep when it happened. He's okay."

Nancy Taylor's husband, Alexander, was known offshore as Ronnie the Rocket because he was in perpetual motion. He was due home that afternoon. A neighbor rapped on her door just after six and said Piper Alpha just blew up. "Ronnie's home today," she said. "He'll be fine."

Maureen Henderson's husband, Dave, had just been promoted to assistant driller and transferred to Piper Alpha from Claymore a week ago. Their first baby was due in four days. Dave was due home in three. Maureen told all of this to the sad man who came to her door after she spent the morning refusing to believe that Dave had anything to do with the pictures on her television set.

Kay Harney, Eddie Crowden's girlfriend, was just getting up to go to work in Portlethen when Eddie's sister called and told her to turn on the television. Fifteen minutes later, Kay was on the road north to the Aberdeen hospital, thinking that if he was alive she would marry him right away.

When the social worker at the door told Don Reid's wife that he was dead, she began to scream. A half hour later, still hysterical but speaking words instead of raw agony, she told the woman who had stayed with her that Don hated Piper Alpha more than all the rigs he had worked on as an Oxy production manager. "It was rotten. He and his men worked around the clock just to keep it running."

The policeman who came to Bill Barron's house drove him to the Skean Dhu Hotel, leaving Trish to wait for what Bill promised would be a phone call soon to come pick him up again. She couldn't believe she'd let him walk out the door, but she did. The Skean Dhu had long been a halfway house for offshore men, a rambling, hard-used,

Marriott-like motel with a hundred rooms, a bar, and a restaurant. Barron walked into the Skean Dhu dining room where about twenty uninjured survivors were waiting with several men from Occidental, a few policemen, and a team of social workers. He heard shouting across the lobby. Two women, the wife and girlfriend of the same man from what they were saying, were looking for him at the hotel. They had been told at the hospital that he had survived. The women shrieked until one of the hotel desk men got between them, then stood in opposite corners of the room, their arms folded against their chests, glaring. Bill Barron watched until he felt a sadness he could not bear. He turned and walked into the dining room to get whatever it was Oxy and the cops wanted finished so he could go home.

Trish came to get him at two in the afternoon after he had given his statement. The police wanted to know how he got off the rig, what he saw of others trying to get off, where he had been when the fire started, what he thought might have happened. The Oxy man asked the same questions, gave him a packet of cash for incidentals, and a duffel bag of clothes. Barron told him he didn't need the cash or the clothes. The Oxy man insisted that he take it. The social worker asked him if he wanted to talk. He had no heart for any of it, but questioning authority was not in his makeup. He left thinking that all these years he had been going offshore there was a warehouse at Dyce full of duffel bags of clothes because somebody knew that it was only a matter of time before this happened.

Eighteen

HELLFIGHTER

Television stations all over Scotland canceled regular programs and kept the news on all day. Reporters looked into the camera with stricken expressions and recited the latest figures. Seventeen men confirmed dead, including two from the *Sandhaven*'s Z-boat. A hundred and thirty men missing with little hope that they would be found alive. Sixty-two survivors, one of them near death in the hospital, more than half severely injured. Ending agonizing speculation by hundreds of families, an extra afternoon edition of the Aberdeen *Press and Journal* carried the names of the confirmed dead and missing. The Grampian police set up a morgue in a hangar at the airport to which the helicopters brought the bodies. By the middle of the afternoon, most of the hundreds of people from the morning at the hospital crowded into the Skean Dhu and the airport parking lots to be near what was left of their men.

In Los Angeles, on the afternoon of July 6, Armand Hammer got word that the trouble on Piper Alpha had become the worst oil rig disaster in history. He called the Occidental hangar at Burbank airport and told his pilots to prepare *Oxy One* for the flight to Aberdeen. The plane was a Boeing 727 with an interior like a yacht, but it would have to make a refueling stop on its long flight across America and the Atlantic. Hammer was at least twenty-four hours from where he wanted to be. He then dictated a statement over the phone to his public relations office in London, which was fully awake at four in the morning U.K. time.

I wish to extend my deepest sympathy to the families of the men who have been injured or lost their lives in this tragic accident. We will continue to do everything we can to help the injured and their families. We have established a task force to assist police in the Aberdeen area and the families of our employees there. A fleet of NATO ships and six helicopters with a medical team are assisting in the search and weather conditions are described as favorable. A team of Occidental executives from California and from our London office are already at the scene working in the rescue effort. All available vessels in the area are assisting in the search for the workers who are missing.

Before leaving Los Angeles, Hammer called oil well firefighter Red Adair to ask for help. Adair said he was already busy. Hammer pleaded with him to drop whatever he was doing and personally help him put out the fires on Piper Alpha. He told Adair that the loss of the rig and shutdown of Claymore and Tartan was costing him five million a day and cutting Great Britain's entire North Sea oil production by 15 percent. Workers on dozens of other North Sea rigs were quitting in wildcat strikes to protest unsafe conditions offshore and production could drop another 25 percent. Piper Alpha was a disaster for Occidental, but it could very quickly turn into a national emergency for England. The nation's losses in taxes and its royalty share of the oil amounted to more than a million a day just with Piper Alpha, Claymore, and Tartan off-line. Everyone was stricken by the loss of life, Hammer said, but he had moved on from tragedy more times than he could count. Occidental's future could not begin until the fires were out and the bodies of the missing men found.

Adair said, "I'm seventy-three years old, Doctor."

"Bullshit," Hammer replied. "I'm ninety. Meet me in Aberdeen."

Eighteen hours after Hammer called him, Adair and his two best men were in Aberdeen. Adair was still vital but with nowhere near the reaction times he needed to survive in harm's way on a burning oil rig. Brian Krause and Ray Henry would be his eyes and ears on a reconnaissance to the rig. They would then follow his orders to direct a full crew of divers and roughnecks to extinguish the fires and cap the wells. At Oxy headquarters, the company's global drilling boss, Leon Daniels, told Adair what little he knew from the television film and the interviews of survivors at the Skean Dhu. There had been a series of explosions that lasted an hour, killed an unknown number of men, and left the tattered ends of the wells and pipes burning on the surface surrounded by wreckage.

That afternoon, a vagrant midsummer gale roared across the North Sea with winds of eighty miles an hour, keeping Adair and his crew in Aberdeen. The next morning, Friday, July 8, they took off in a chopper to look at the remains of Piper Alpha. Circling the scene, Adair saw that most of the platform was gone. The heavy steel firewalls of A Module and the drilling floor had protected the hunk of the rig that remained intact. It was twisted and blackened by the intense heat with flames roaring out of the wellheads. A hundred feet away across open water, the pipeline risers sent columns of blue-white and orange flame into the sky, which was now a low slate-gray cloud cover with a good wind kicking up below. The rig was still shedding parts of itself as pockets of explosive fluids and gas erupted sending chunks of metal sizzling into the sea.

Adair's most celebrated well kill, the one on which *Hellfighters* had been based, was called the Devil's Cigarette Lighter in the media. For weeks, the blown-out Libyan well sent an eight-hundred-foot column of flame into the sky over the Sahara Desert that John Glenn saw from his orbiting Mercury capsule. Piper Alpha looked worse. Adair had to put out the fires, then seal the wells 475 feet underwater. Nobody had ever drilled for oil at that depth. Nobody had ever capped a well down there, either.

After a few dismal passes around the burning wreckage, Adair told his helicopter pilot to land on *Tharos,* which was anchored a mile away from Piper Alpha. It was still the control center for search and rescue operations. Adair introduced himself to Captain Letty, asked permission to set up his command post on *Tharos,* and returned to shore for the night. At the airport after his reconnaissance, Adair stood at a podium in the Occidental departure lounge and talked to reporters.

"How this happened, God only knows," Adair said. "I've been

fighting oil rig fires for fifty years and it's the worst thing I've ever
seen. Ask the people of Aberdeen to say a prayer for us."

The next day, the third since Piper Alpha blew up, Letty eased
Tharos to the upwind side of the rig near enough so its 350-ton
crane projected over the wreckage. Adair, Krause, and Henry went
to work. The wind had dropped, but not much. A leftover chop on
a six-foot swell made maneuvering in close quarters extremely dangerous, but the time for taking risks had not ended. Before divers
and robot subs could comb the seafloor for bodies, they had to know
more about what was happening underwater and on the wreck of
the rig. From the boom of the crane, Krause and Henry swung over
the smoldering steel in a wire basket and landed on Piper Alpha's
remains. With *Tharos* and *Maersk Cutter* playing streams of water
over the wreckage like covering fire in battle, Krause and Henry
inspected the devastation. Intense heat had disfigured everything.
Steel jutted at sharp and deadly angles, all of it slick with waxy oil.
Nothing had purpose. No flat surfaces remained. They first looked
around for bodies but saw none. Tying themselves to the rig and to
each other with safety lines, Krause and Henry separated debris one
piece at a time, picking their way through the wreckage to the tops
of the blown-out wellheads. The roar of the fires made radio communication impossible. To lift the heavier pieces of steel blocking
their way, they guided *Tharos*'s crane with hand signals.

While Krause and Henry worked on the rig, divers braved patches
of burning oil and deadly debris on the surface to inspect the platform underwater. They found oil and gas gushing from many of
Piper Alpha's wells, which were sheared off hundreds of feet down.
Several more wellheads were spewing burning gas and oil from two
separate places on the surface. The gas pipelines connecting Claymore, Tartan, and MCP-01 had been shut down, and blowing out
their fire with explosives was going to be straightforward. After
that, Adair and his crew were looking at weeks of work to extinguish the runaway oil wells and cap them with cement in a tech-
nique known as a top kill. It was a little like plugging a drain with
a mixture that had to be liquid enough to flow through a hose but
thick enough to staunch the flow of the oil.

In Aberdeen, Adair lumbered off the chopper and briefed the

press on the dismal situation offshore. The Lord Provost of the city stood next to him. After Adair told the reporters that it would be many days before the fires would be out, one of them asked the Lord Provost how Adair and his team would be compensated.

"I think the attitude here is 'give him a check and let him fill in the numbers.' "

Seventy-two hours after the first explosions on Piper Alpha, two dozen ships and a squadron of Z-boats had found just seventeen bodies. There were sixty-two survivors, half of them still in the hospital. An ungodly 147 were still missing. The Saturday morning edition of the Aberdeen *Press and Journal* captured the misery of the dreadful uncertainty that had taken over the city. In a sidebar the wife of one of the missing men was quoted, "Yesterday we were hoping for a life. Now we are just hoping for a body."

The newspaper headlines were like bells tolling over a small-town funeral. UNBORN BABE WILL NOT SEE DAD. FAMILY COMFORTS BRIDE OF SEVEN WEEKS. LIFE-LONG FRIENDS DIED TOGETHER. Every day seemed worse than the day before it. For two weeks, the papers and television news intoned the names of the dead and cheered on Red Adair, who was still out there with his crew trying to put out the fire. For every day they could work, the weather drove them off the wreckage for three. When Adair gave interviews, he pronounced Piper Alpha the most dangerous, difficult fire he had ever fought.

Most of all, the newspaper and television reporters asked the one question everyone wanted answered: Why did Piper Alpha blow up? By Saturday, Occidental public relations was saying that interviews with survivors and film of the disaster taken by the Grampian Television crew indicated that the first explosion was in either the gas compression C Module or the oil production B Module on the production deck.

"It was a gas-type explosion," John Brading, Oxy International's president, said from his office in Aberdeen. "We do not know how or where it started. I am sorry to say that there is little hope that any of the missing men will be found alive." Brading kept talking. "Anyone in the Occidental team would have derived tremendous pride from our record over twelve years of operation from that platform. That pride has been destroyed in the last few hours."

As a counterpoint to the abject misery of the real news, the television stations and newspapers ran film and photographs of the steady stream of dignitaries coming to Aberdeen that weekend. *Silver Pit* limped into the harbor, her flanks charred and blistered. Her crew lined up on the dock for congratulations from Prince Charles and Lady Diana. George Carson, looking like he hadn't slept in a week, smiled at Lady Di like he was chatting her up in a bar. Prime Minister Margaret Thatcher spent a half hour at the hospital with survivors and pledged to the families of the lost that the full might of the nation would be brought to bear on ending the uncertainty about the missing men. Armand Hammer, who left the media and the details to Brading, spent a morning at the hospital. Frocked in an antiseptic gown, he posed for photographs with Mark Reid, Erland Grieve, Bob Carey, and anyone else who wanted to meet him.

The next day, thousands of people filled St. Machar's Church of Scotland Cathedral in downtown Aberdeen and spilled out into the surrounding ancient graveyard in which loudspeakers had been set up. In a voice that boomed through the granite canyon of Union Street and down cobbled lanes to the waterfront, the preacher asked for prayers. "For those who waited by the telephone for the call that never came. For those who scanned survival lists in the hospital for names that were not there. For the wife whose husband would never again tell her that he loved her. For parents who had lost not only a son but all their dreams. For the poor souls holding hope against hope that their beloved would be found alive." After the sermon, a bishop told the congregation: "Aberdeen is a sad city, but a city not broken by sadness."

Between that Sunday and the National Day of Mourning on Wednesday, July 20, divers using robot submarines with grappling arms picked up the bodies of twenty more men from the bottom of the sea. Above, Adair and his crew now numbered more than thirty men and two ships. They made enough progress to let the divers and ROVs search for the dead underwater. One hundred and twenty-nine men were still missing. The wreckage was still on fire. Adair and Hammer stopped talking to the press.

During the two weeks since Ed Punchard flew home to Cornwall, Vicky, and Suzie, he had bound his invisible wounds with manic energy. He didn't sleep more than two hours at a time and woke in the same hyperactive state he had been in since the moment of the first explosion on Piper Alpha. During his first week at home, he heard a bang in the night and leaped into the air clutching the duvet around him. Vicky grabbed his ankle. "It's okay, Ed. It's just the lifeboat alarm. The boat's been called out. It's okay. Come back to bed."

When Punchard was awake, during the day or night, he was obsessed with what he now believed was his mission in life as a survivor of the world's worst oil rig disaster: To inform as many people as possible that financial cutbacks and the system of awarding offshore contracts for fixed prices had led to unsafe working conditions in the North Sea. Before Piper, he had been concerned about the inequities of the oil boom. Now he was obsessed. As a survivor, with his picture in the newspapers and on television, he had access to the media, members of Parliament, and trade union leaders. Punchard was furious when one of the tabloid papers reported that "Dr. Hammer, who flew from Los Angeles to Aberdeen for a briefing on the tragedy, said the grieving families will get £100,000 each and pensions for life." The truth was that only the thirty-one families of men directly employed by Occidental were offered the money. The families of men who worked for the contractors got none of the Occidental payoff.

Punchard went berserk when he heard that the day after the catastrophe, Occidental and the British government announced that each was giving £1 million to a public trust fund to which citizens could also contribute. The money would be paid out to help the families of the dead and the injured and to finance research into ways of preventing such a disaster from happening again. For years, men who worked offshore had been raging about safety and dreadful working conditions on the rigs. It was already the duty of the government and the oil giants to do the research and to solve those problems. Why should hardworking people be donating their shillings and fivers instead of the people who are making all the money from the oil fields that are killing men. Punchard threw the tabloid on the floor and got on the telephone. He called every journalist who had interviewed him and raged. He called the trade unions and railed at them because what few men they represented offshore were getting shafted. He called the office of the Secretary of State for Energy, Cecil Parkinson, and was startled when Parkinson's secretary called him back to invite him to his office for a meeting on July 18. The memorial service for the victims of Piper Alpha was scheduled for July 20. Punchard accepted Parkinson's invitation. He scheduled a meeting earlier the same day with the Professional Divers Association to work on the plan for recovering the bodies from Piper Alpha.

Punchard marched into the divers meeting and took over. He scanned the recommendation that priority be given to the recovery of the bodies and the accommodation module by navy divers and tossed it to the table like it was a badly written student essay.

"This is wrong. The navy divers may be very good in their way, but they don't know what an oil rig is," Punchard ranted, unable to stop himself even though he could see that he was rocking the others back in their chairs. "Why involve the Royal Navy when there's a wealth of talent and expertise already available? Within hours, you could assemble a group of North Sea divers who would've already worked on Piper and would know exactly what the rig looked like underwater and how to find their way around an accommodation module in which they'd actually lived. Furthermore, under no circumstances can divers go straight into the submerged accommodation module. It has to be treated like any other diving job. You start at the top and clear off the debris because you can't work beneath something that's likely to come crashing down on you. Once the area's been cleared, the bodies and the module can be recovered. You cannot do it before. It would be insane to risk unnecessarily the lives of divers while recovering Piper's dead."

When Punchard stopped talking, the air flowed back into the room but nobody spoke for a long minute. Finally, the head of the divers' union proposed a rewritten recommendation. "The recovery of bodies will be undertaken as a major priority as soon as the structure is made safe."

Two hours later, Punchard was still steaming when he walked into a wainscoted conference room furnished with antiques at the Department of Energy. After an assistant settled him and three trade union leaders at the table, Parkinson, his junior minister, Peter Morrison, and a half dozen other men in starched white shirts and dark suits walked in. As they circled the table shaking hands, Punchard thought, This looks like a scene from *Yes, Minister,* a popular television spoof of the British government. He choked back a laugh before realizing how completely out of his element he was among these people. They seemed so calm. So in control. For the first fifteen minutes, Punchard collapsed into silence as though a switch had been thrown somewhere inside him. He felt afraid to speak, afraid that what he was going to say would sound unsophisticated or simpleminded. Then it occurred to him: If you can climb down that rope on a blazing oil rig and not be scared, Ed Punchard, what the hell are you worried about here?

One union guy said that men were afraid to come forward to talk about unsafe practices. Parkinson spoke so softly that everyone in the room leaned toward him. He pointed out that his department had an anonymous phone line for reporting problems like that.

Punchard felt himself flow seamlessly back into his anger. "I have no doubt that you believe there is a system," he said on the edge of shouting. "I have no doubt that when your civil servants made this provision their intention was to stop victimization taking place. But we cannot talk about it in this manner. We have to accept that the system doesn't work. Believe me, people are too scared to come forward. So the real question that must be addressed is, What would it take to make people come forward? The answer is a new system. You have to scrap the existing system."

One of the bureaucrats pointedly asked Punchard if he could provide any proof of victimization of men who blow the whistle on tatty rigs and unsafe work practices.

"No problem," Punchard said, and launched into his own story of life as a baby diver afraid to speak out for fear of never finding work again. He railed about fixed-price contracts, shoddy work, fudged inspections, and the culture of blame-laying and secrecy off-shore. One of the union guys cut him off and looked at his watch. Parkinson took the last word, promising only that the inquiry into Piper Alpha would be thorough and unbiased. He was appointing Scottish judge Douglas Cullen to chair a public inquiry into the disaster. Parkinson also guaranteed that he would spare no effort or expense to recover all the bodies from Piper Alpha. As Parkinson left the room, he reached out to shake Punchard's hand, looked at the identity badge Punchard had been issued when he came in, identifying him as a survivor. "Ah," the minister said, "I understand."

For two weeks, Vicky had tiptoed around her husband, aware that the shock of what had happened to him was going to leave scars but that he would heal. As Ed was shutting her out, she dipped into their reservoir of marital goodwill to accept it. She hoped that going back to Aberdeen for the memorial would be a turning point, that things might at least begin to get back to normal, whatever normal was going to be for what was left of their lives. She calmed Ed when a car backfiring sent him into a panic. She listened to him when he talked about feeling like he was one of the shell-shocked World War I grandfathers in his childhood neighborhood who blinked uncontrollably or cringed at any sound remotely like gunfire. He tried to reach out from wherever he had gone and told Vicky over and over that it was her and Suzie he thought of when he was being dragged through the sea by *Silver Pit*. He said that most of the men who survived said it was their women who inspired them to fight for life in their worst moments of torment and fear. Despite Ed's spoken gratitude, he was living on another planet, one filled with rage and terror. Vicky was sure that seeing some of the other survivors in Aberdeen would help. The day before they left, she was glad when he told her he was definitely going to visit Eric Brianchon in the hospital. The compassion she saw in Ed's face was the most alive he had been except for the anger.

At Heathrow airport the day after the meeting with the energy minister, Ed left Vicky and Suzie to guard their place in the check-in line while he went to the newsstand to buy some French-language magazines for Brianchon. He told Vicky that Eric probably hadn't had too many visitors being so far from home. He'd appreciate something to read. Five minutes later, Punchard was back with an armload of magazines as their turn came to check in. Vicky and Suzie wandered over the gift shop while he took care of business. The woman at the counter looked at his name on the reservation and connected his face with the pictures she had seen in the newspapers.

"What a terrible experience you must have had, Mr. Punchard."

Punchard nodded.

"Wasn't it sad," she said, "that the poor Frenchman died this morning?"

Ed grimaced and stared at the woman like she had slapped him. "What?" She realized that Punchard was hearing the news for the first time from her. "Oh, I'm so, so sorry. I didn't mean to upset you. Was he a friend of yours?"

"No, not a friend," Punchard said. "I was just one of the people who rescued him."

By the time Punchard found Vicky in the gift shop, he was sobbing, a deep, throaty rasp he was helpless to contain. "What on earth has happened?" Vicky asked. "Eric Brianchon died." Punchard was inconsolable. By the time they reached the jetway to board their flight, he had stopped crying but fell into a brooding silence. As Vicky wrangled her rambunctious daughter into her seat, she understood that her husband and her family were far more grievously wounded by what had happened to him than she had imagined.

The memorial service in Aberdeen was echoed in remembrances all over the United Kingdom on what Margaret Thatcher had declared a day of national morning. Only in Aberdeen did the sadness coalesce into agony. Two thousand dark-cloaked people packed the cathedral and flowed out into the surrounding streets. About half the survivors came, some alone, some with their families; others were still in the hospital. Armand Hammer and Red Adair arrived and sat in the back of the church with a hundred or so other men and women who worked for Occidental. Cecil Parkinson was among the last to arrive, taking a seat behind the survivors. Bill, Trish, and Melanie Barron were there. Mark and Mary Reid with their son, Marc. John Barr. Geoff Bollands. Fred Busby. Harry Calder. Bob Carey. Dick Common. Ian Fowler. Barry Goodwin. Michael Jennings. Mahmood Khan. David Kinrade. Ian Letham. The loved ones of dead men filled the rest of the church, wives, children, sweethearts, cousins, friends, and neighbors. Ann Gillanders, her daughter, Yvonne, and son, Evan, Ian's father and mother, and two sisters. Two hundred friends and relatives of the six men named Duncan who died—Alexander, Charles, Eric, John, Thomas, and William. Women crushed by the deaths of their beloveds slumped in the pews mourning Colin Seaton, Alan Carter, Eddie Crowden, Harold Flook, George Fowler, Brian Lithgow, Michael Scorgie, Robert Argo Vernon. Other men whose names were listed alphabetically in the bulletin printed for the service testified that Piper Alpha was a Scottish tragedy. McBoyle. McCall. McCleod. McCulloch. McDonald. McElwee. McEwan. McGregor. McGurk. McIntosh. McKay. McLaughlin. McPake. McWhinnie. McWilliams.

Bob Ballantyne and Pat Slater didn't show up. He didn't want to be in the same room with people from Occidental and the British government who he was passionately convinced were to blame for what had happened on Piper Alpha. Instead, Ballantyne took an armful of flowers to a beach north of the city and threw them into the sea.

Andrew Wylie, a Church of Scotland preacher appointed by his bishop as the chaplain to the oil industry, took the pulpit and said, "We are here to remember those who died on Piper Alpha." Sobs and wretched gasps rebounded off the vaulted granite walls, sounds so awful and sad that Wylie did not get another word out for minutes. He just stood there, crying himself, looking down at thousands of broken hearts, knowing that the comfort he was there to offer would do nothing to mend them. Most of the faces he saw still carried not only the grief of dreadful loss but also the visceral uncertainty of not having seen a body, without which they could not begin to heal. Two weeks after the explosion, the remains of Piper Alpha still smoldered. A hundred and forty men were still missing.

Nineteen

SADNESS

Scottish women had been losing their men to the oceans for centuries, but Piper Alpha was worse because they couldn't get away from it. Each day's newspaper carried photographs of funerals until there were no more bodies. The silence of those still missing was hideous. Everyone in the city knew a man who had died, a survivor who was living with the nightmares of what he had seen, or someone who was asking God for the unspeakable. That the body of a son, husband, father, or beloved would be found.

A week after the memorial service, Red Adair and his men finally extinguished the flames of Piper Alpha's wells and began capping them. For a week, they pumped cement through hoses from specially tanked ships on the surface, guided by robot submarines with television cameras. Adair had capped underwater wells, but never at this depth. He told the media that he hoped he'd never have to do it again.

On the smoking wreckage of the rig, Adair's crew probed for bodies. They found none. With the fires out, divers and robot submarines plotted grids on the seafloor and began their search for the accommodation module. They knew about where it had hit the water on the east side of the rig, but the vagrancy of the ocean currents during its descent to the bottom made its final resting place uncertain. On August 8, a robot sub tethered to a diving bell sent back pictures of what looked like a four-story building resting upside down on the bottom of the sea. On the video images the sub transmitted to the surface, the enormous object looked like a dark hump in the seafloor against the diffused remnants of sunlight filtering from above. The floodlights of the sub panned over it, revealing four decks of staterooms, offices, and the galley that were once 170 feet above the sea at the top of Piper Alpha. There was no doubt. It was the main living quarters. Two hundred yards to the north, the video showed a smaller rectangular object about the size of eight railway boxcars, the additional accommodation block that had been attached to the main module before they separated during the plunge from the rig.

Occidental and the Royal Navy gave in to Ed Punchard's insistence that North Sea divers recover the bodies in the living quarters and prepare the modules to be lifted to the surface. From hundreds of volunteers, one of the diving contractors put together four teams to probe the wreckage. With the help of remote-controlled cameras and retriever arms, they would recover as many bodies as they could, then attach cables to lift the 1,100-ton main module and the 110-ton additional module. The job was going to take weeks. Working in shifts around the clock whenever the currents were not too dangerous, the divers left their saturation chambers on the deck of a barge and descended in pairs in pressurized bells. They swam out through an airlock into the dark ocean, orienting themselves from memorized blueprints. The smaller module was laying with its doors and windows facing the bottom. They could find no way in, so one team of divers went to work rigging it for the lift.

The main living quarters lay on its top, with one corner buried deep in the seafloor. The bottom, where it had been torn from the rest of Piper Alpha, was scorched and scarred by explosion and fire. Some of the struts that once bound it to the rig had melted into slag and twisted steel. A tangle of railings and catwalks draped two sides of the giant box where the doors once were. On another side, the divers could see through glassless window frames, but going inside was much too dangerous. Instead, they sent the robots in to videotape the collapsed walls, ceilings, and steel plates. Everything buoyant had risen to the top in the upside-down wreckage, forming a layer of impenetrable debris. On the third day of diving, they retrieved seven corpses in life vests and survival suits that were in the canteen within reach of the windows. The divers brought each body to their diving bell, then left it there when they entered the airlock to their saturation chambers. On the barge, medics zipped the dead into black plastic bags and put them on choppers for the flight to the morgue in the hangar at Aberdeen airport. The divers could see many more bodies in the canteen and stairwells, but bringing them out was impossible, even using the robots. With the dead waiting inside, the divers turned to the work of attaching bolts and cables to raise the tomb from the sea.

At the end of August, Occidental chartered the most powerful floating crane on the North Sea to lift the accommodation module to a barge that would be towed to the Occidental wharf at the oil terminal at Flotta in the Orkney Islands. The McDermott Derrick Barge 102 was a 551-foot-long, 319-foot-wide steel platform on pontoons that could be ballasted with seawater to stabilize it. The DB-102 was propelled by six three-thousand-horsepower, computer-controlled diesel thrusters, could carry a construction crew of up to 750 men, and lay pipelines up to sixty inches in diameter. It was equipped with decompression chambers, dive gas reservoirs, and an array of tethered and autonomous robot submarines. It had two cranes that together could lift up to 12,000 tons. The barge and its crew cost Occidental $250,000 a day. By the middle of September, divers finished welding and bolting a web of cables to the accommodation module. When the cranes on the DB-102 lifted the load a few feet from the bottom, one of the cables snapped. The huge box spun and slammed back to the bottom, clouding the water column with silt that killed the visibility and took hours to dissipate.

Back in Aberdeen, social worker Archie Robb had become the media spokesman at the morgue. He delivered the news that it would be at least another three weeks before the bodies of the men inside the sunken living quarters would come home. Dealing with the media had been a frightening challenge for Robb. He was constantly afraid he would say something indelicate about the dead men that might increase the suffering of their loved ones.

For a month after the first attempt to lift the accommodation module, weekly gales reminded everyone that autumn had come to the North Sea. Between storms, the divers and the cranes maneuvered a massive steel slab underneath the living quarters to support it during the immensely stressful lift from so great a depth. To each corner of the slab, they fixed cables to eye bolts, hoping the whole thing would hold together long enough to reach the surface. The lift took twenty hours. Nobody aboard DB-102 or any of the three ships standing watch over the remains of Piper Alpha slept. On the deck of the crane barge, the chief constable of the Grampian regional police force, Alistair Lynn, and detective superintendent Alistair Richie watched Piper Alpha's living quarters break the surface at sunset the next day. Lynn and Richie were Scotland's honor guard to accompany the dead to Flotta where they would lead teams of other policemen in removing the bodies.

By the last week in October, Piper Alpha's living quarters was a blackened, rusting scar against the slate winter sky on the dock at Flotta. For the first week, television camera crews, photographers, and reporters braved the bumpy flights between Aberdeen and Orkney, then left Alistair Lynn and his policemen to their work. Twenty officers came north, most of them from Aberdeen, all of them volunteers who had been told that their job inside the accommodation module was going to be the worst thing they would ever do in their lives. Lynn's second-in-command, Ian Gordon, recruited Dr. David Alexander, a psychologist at the University of Aberdeen, to come with the policemen to Orkney. He lived with them in the Occidental housing, ate with them, and listened to them talk about what they saw and felt. The officers divided themselves into four teams of five men each, giving themselves three days off for every one they spent retrieving bodies.

The four decks of the accommodation module had collapsed into heaps of steel, wallboard, furniture, plastic paneling, wires, and aluminum ducting, all of it smoke-blackened and oozing with the muck of being submerged in saltwater for four months. Inside, the air was fetid. Only the canteen was recognizable as a room.

The search took five weeks. By the end of it, the policemen had extracted eighty-seven more bodies. The conditions of the dead

ranged from pristine to unrecognizable depending on where the
victims had been when the explosion of the Claymore riser blew
the module from Piper Alpha. The most likely to be in good shape
were those men wearing just underwear or pajamas who had been
asleep in bed. Most of those they found in the canteen had died of
asphyxiation, their bodies torn and ruined during the plunge. Some
bodies were barely recognizable as human, much like what some
of the searchers had seen on duty at plane crashes and car wrecks.
Some were so badly damaged that they were never identified. After
cremation, their ashes were marked "Unknown."

Inside the accommodation module, some of the policemen
armored themselves. "When I go in there," one of them told Alexander, "as far as I'm concerned I'm going into a spaceship to look
for Martians."

Some of the other policemen dealt with their chore by talking to
the dead. "Right, laddie," one of them said when he pulled wreckage away to expose another corpse. "Let's get you home."

In Aberdeen, the funerals began again. Each of them freshened the
wounds of families who had deluded themselves with hope that their
men would come home alive. Some of them were stoic affairs, but
most were burdened with so much unreasonable tragedy that grace
was elusive. It was impossible to summon condolence worthy of the
grief. The funerals tore open the hearts of those who thought they
had already accepted the deaths of their loved ones. Many survivors
attended the gravesides of men they hardly knew. Ed Punchard and
Vicky went to several, among the few times since the memorial service in late July when they were together. Punchard was lost in his
obsession about North Sea safety. He spent as much time in Aberdeen as he did in Cornwall with his family. He went to meetings on
the absurdly meager settlements Occidental was offering to families
and survivors, the trust fund to add to those settlements, and preparations for the public hearings on the disaster. He was furious that
they weren't going to start until after the new year.

At home, Punchard's marriage unraveled. During the three

months since Piper Alpha, he had spiraled into distraction, obsession, uncontrollable anger, and silence. A few days after the memorial service in Aberdeen, he and Vicky were watching an after-dinner television documentary about the Korean War in which a bomb explodes with graphic aftermath. Debris fell from surrounding buildings, blood streamed down the shocked faces of people rushing from the scene. Punchard was right back on the sixty-eight-foot level of Piper Alpha. He saw it more clearly than what was on the television screen. An injured man was being carried down metal stairs. Another man appeared with blood all over him, begging for help. Punchard wanted to help, but he couldn't move his legs or arms. He then saw Suzie playing on the carpet at their feet, saw Vicky with that rapt expression of concentration on her face that he adored, but he was incapable of being in their world. He heard cars speeding past the window, cups rattling in the kitchen, the cat purring on his lap. Punchard felt like he had to make a decision about where he wanted to be but he only returned to the living when the images of the rig finally faded on their own like a withering mirage. Vicky shook his arm. "Ed. Ed. Are you all right?" He snapped at her. "Leave me be. I'm fine."

Punchard always had a worm of anger in him that was easily awakened. The world should be fair. Everything about Piper Alpha was unfair. He and Vicky bickered constantly. He was impatient with friends who incensed him when they suggested that it had been months since the accident and didn't he think he should be moving on. He was absolutely sure that his life depended on holding on to the intense focus and motivation that had saved him when *Silver Pit* was dragging him through the water. He gave in to adrenaline rushes that lasted for days before collapsing into listlessness and angry irritation. In either state, Punchard took absurd risks. He passed a truck on a two-lane curve with Suzie in her car seat beside him.

Vicky watched her husband deteriorate, shut out from his pain and unable to offer him solace. Their marriage had been fragile before Piper Alpha. A new baby had stressed it even further. Now their life together looked hopeless to her. Ed did not care about anything but the injustice of Piper Alpha.

The one person who made sense to Punchard was Vicky's father, Mike Laloë. He had been a Japanese prisoner of war and survived when his prison ship was torpedoed. He didn't expect Punchard to be normal. Laloë told Punchard that many prisoners wrote books after surviving the war and it helped some of them come to terms with what had happened. Mike had an office on the Falmouth docks and he offered Ed a desk in one corner at a window overlooking the harbor. Laloë suggested that while Ed dredged up his feelings to put them down on paper it might be a good idea if he talked to a psychiatrist who specialized in his kind of wounds. Punchard didn't resist. He believed in seeking professional advice. If you wanted to learn to drive, it made sense to go to a driving instructor. If you were being sued, you hired a lawyer. He went hopefully to his first appointment. It was almost his last. The first question the psychiatrist asked was, "Well, what's wrong with you then?"

By the end of the session, the psychiatrist told Punchard he clearly was suffering from what he called post-traumatic stress disorder. It was a way of understanding emotional trauma that had gotten considerable attention in the psychiatric journals in England after men returned from the Falklands War in shock that led them to suicide, alcoholism, and marital discord. The literature described patterns of behavior that ended the victims' lives as surely as a hand grenade.

"People normally try to construct for themselves a life that is predictable," the psychiatrist said. "They feather their nest and have around them their partner and family. But it is an illusion of predictability they have created. People who have a major traumatic shock, no matter how well they cope with it at the time, experience a massive turn-around in their life. Previously, life was thought to be predictable. Suddenly, it is known to be unpredictable. The premise of life and existence has been changed."

Hearing that he had profound injuries that were invisible to the rest of the world did not heal Punchard. He developed a tic in his left eye that made him look like he was punctuating every word he said with a wink. He came within inches of a head-on collision on the road. He raged at meetings about claims by Occidental that nobody had smelled gas before the explosion. He barked at his family. Just before Christmas, Vicky took Suzie and left him.

Six weeks after Bill Barron survived the world's deadliest oil rig disaster without a scratch, he was drinking and digging in the front yard of his cottage near the River Don north of Aberdeen. This went on for months until his wife, Trish, gave him an ultimatum: Stop drinking and digging or I'm taking our daughter and leaving you. Barron agreed to attend some of the meetings of the survivors' support group. He went to his first session, sat quietly in the back of the room, and said nothing. Other men told their stories about getting off the rig, being in the hospital, the men they left behind, their guilt, their anger at Occidental, Piper Alpha, the world. He shook hands with men he hadn't seen since the Skean Dhu Hotel. They all said the same thing to him. "I'm glad you got off." Just that. "I'm glad you got off."

Barron listened as their stories spilled into the room in torrents of sadness and regret. Finally, he tried to tell his own truth about the night of fire. He wanted to talk about the new guy, the guy whose name he couldn't remember when he almost went through the fire into the White House to look for him. Barron failed, waving his hand in front of his face and choking back anguished sobs. A few nights later, he tried again. Spoke the dead boy's name. Shaun Glendinning. Barron kept going to meetings, retreating into silence most of the time, but the drinking and digging stopped. He was better, but not good. He swung from hours of frantic energy into days of silence. Trish stopped expecting him to ever be anyone but a tired, strange old man at fifty-five and just loved him. Barron decided he would never go offshore again. He had no idea what to do with what was left of his life.

The Piper Alpha Families and Survivors Association commissioned a permanent memorial to the dead in Aberdeen, a place to which families and survivors could come for a measure of peace that a monument can sometimes inspire. Armand Hammer had agreed to pay settlements ranging from $52,000 to $1,750,000. He said he would fight the battalions of lawyers who had filed suit against the corporation claiming billions more. When the association asked Occidental in Aberdeen for money to commission the memorial, Hammer passed down the word to say no. The company had already donated a leather-bound book of remembrance to the Aberdeen City Art Gallery. That was enough.

The association set up a fund for public giving that swelled to $175,000 in six months with contributions from other oil companies, families, schools, and coin boxes on shop counters. It was enough for the kind of monument they wanted to build.

In spring of 1989, after the most dreadful winter of sadness in Aberdeen's memory, a twenty-eight-year-old artist from the Black Isle Peninsula north of Inverness emerged as the front-runner to design the memorial. The slim, almost frail, hauntingly dark-eyed woman with spiked orange hair was an unlikely but perfect fit for the job. For ten years, Sue Jane Taylor had been painting, drawing, and photographing the men and machines of North Sea oil. In 1987, Occidental allowed her to spend a few days on Piper Alpha. She took hundreds of photographs and sketched herself into exhaustion.

A year later, on the night Piper Alpha exploded, Taylor had been in her apartment in London. She heard the news on the radio. Her first thoughts were of the men she had met during her days on the rig. She couldn't imagine any survivors at all from the inferno she saw on the television. A few weeks later, Taylor got a phone call from Occidental's head of public relations, a nice fellow who had been helpful in arranging her trip to Piper Alpha. He said he heard that she was about to launch a touring retrospective of her prints and photographs of the oil boom in Scotland at the City Art Center in Edinburgh. He would like to talk to her about it as soon as possible. Taylor agreed to meet him at his office the next day, certain that he was going to offer Oxy's support for the exhibition. When she got to his office, she was startled by the transformation the young PR man had undergone. He was wan, terse, obviously under a lot of pressure, and doing something that was distasteful to him. Instead

of promoting Oxy's virtues and achievements to the public, his job
was now to conceal as much about the company, its rigs, and its
workers as possible. With barely contained embarrassment, he said
that Occidental wanted to buy all of her paintings, drawings, notes,
and photographs from Piper Alpha. She could name a price, in
return for canceling the exhibition scheduled to open soon in Edinburgh. Taylor forced herself to take a breath, thinking, Armand
Hammer is reputed to be one of the world's greatest and most phil-
anthropic art patrons in the world and he wants me to cancel an
exhibition? When she could speak, Taylor said she had to get some
advice before answering and stumbled from the office.

Taylor talked to friends. She talked to a lawyer. Obviously, Occidental was preparing to do battle over its liability for what happened
on their rig and feared evidence that could damn the company in
her drawings and photographs. The Piper Alpha settlement offers,
their rejection by the families of the dead and survivors, and the
squads of lawyers descending on Aberdeen were daily fare in the
newspapers. Taylor read that a families and survivors association
had gotten organized in Aberdeen. She decided to go up there and
talk to whomever would speak with her. No one but the men of
Piper Alpha, their widows and children should have anything to say
about whether her work should be exhibited or suppressed.

At the association office in Aberdeen, Taylor ran into Bob Ballantyne. He said he remembered her visit a year ago. She told him she
was glad he got off the rig. Ballantyne said he was glad to be alive,
but he was battling incredible mood swings, alienation, and anger.
He spent most of each day thinking about his last moments on Piper
Alpha before he went into the sea, about drifting and screaming,
about the men who did not get off. He had taken up painting, trying
to banish the demons by putting them in watercolor on paper. Ballantyne told her she should never give in to Oxy. He introduced her
to everyone who came to the office. They all told her the same thing.
Two weeks before the opening, she got a message that Kate Graham
had called from the Occidental office in Aberdeen. Graham wanted
to talk about the exhibition, obviously Oxy's last-ditch effort to
stop it. Taylor didn't return the call.

Taylor had the inside track on the memorial commission, but not

only because she and her work were so naturally entwined with the
survivors and the families. The design she presented for the memorial was very close to what the group sketched out months earlier. A
central bronze figure, twice lifesize, faced north toward the entrance
to a four-acre rose garden in Hazelhead Park north of Aberdeen. In
the figure's left hand, he holds a pool of oil sculpted in the shape of
an unwinding spiral that flows into gold leaf. His right hand points
to the ground, indicating the source of the crude oil. Carved on
his helmet were a fish and a seabird. A second figure faced west,
a depiction of a roustabout representing the physical work of taking oil from the sea. His pose emphasized opposite straining move-
ments, pushing and pulling. On his right sleeve was a Celtic tree of
life, its roots deep in the ground, the tips of its branches reaching to
the sky. The third figure faced east, a young man in a survival suit
representing the spirit of youth that prevails offshore. On his left
sleeve was a stylized osprey, the sea eagle, its head in gold leaf. The
three figures rose fifteen feet from a plinth of granite quarried in
Aberdeen, etched with the names of Piper Alpha's dead and missing.
Sealed in the plinth would be a small casket of ashes from bodies
recovered from the wreckage and marked "Unknown." Taylor had
never done a bronze sculpture. She won the commission anyway.

A few weeks later, facing a nine-month deadline to finish the
monument, Taylor went to a meeting of the survivors and families
to ask for help. She wanted to work from life, not photographs.
With models, she could be sure of capturing angles of arms, legs,
and expressions, the shapes and folds of a survival suit, the exact
posture of a man pushing and pulling. She asked who would be
willing to model for the memorial sculpture. Bill Barron jumped
from his chair and said he'd do it. For months afterward, he drove
an hour each way to the Scottish Sculpture Workshop in Lumsden
where Taylor worked. Day after day, with his spaniel, Biff, at his
feet, Barron stood frozen in the pose of a man offering his hand to
the world. As Taylor worked her pencils, then her plaster, Barron
told her stories of his early life in the army as a guard at the Tower
of London and of the pleasure of building power stations. Over
and over, he told her about his escape from Piper Alpha, about the
screams in the canteen and the White House, about hanging on

the end of the rope and dropping into the North Sea, about his terrible guilt because he had survived and so many other men had died. They talked about the sadness that had already transformed Aberdeen and everyone who lived there forever. He told her about trying to keep Piper Alpha standing with wire and paint, about the shortcuts Oxy took all the time without thinking about the men whose lives depended on the rig. By the time Taylor handed her masterpiece over to the bronze foundry, both of them agreed that what happened to Piper Alpha was a crime and Occidental Petroleum was the criminal.

Twenty

RAGE

Lord William Douglas Cullen opened Great Britain's investigation into the Piper Alpha disaster on January 19, 1989, at the Aberdeen conference center, around the corner from Occidental headquarters north of the city. Except for some squabbling by trade union leaders that the inquiry would probe only the causes of the explosions without addressing what they insisted was a culture of blame and cover-up on the North Sea, Cullen's appointment had been applauded. For most people, Cullen was like a trusted uncle summoned to mediate a virulent family rift. He was a Highlander from Dundee, a fifty-three-year-old judge who had spent most of his career hearing medical claims and patiently rising through the ranks of the judiciary. Cullen was the epitome of a barrister, a sharp-featured, fit, handsome man who brought Gary Cooper to mind and managed not to look ridiculous when he wore his powdered wig in a courtroom. None of the families of the dead or the survivors who would be compelled to testify relished the idea of reliving the worst hours of their lives, but they believed that Cullen was going to get to the truth. He had no power to file criminal complaints if he found negligence, but he could recommend further investigation by prosecutors.

On the first day of the inquiry, Cullen rapped his gavel and read the letter of appointment from Energy Secretary Cecil Parkinson. Cullen then posed the two questions he had been ordered to answer:

"What were the causes and circumstances of the disaster on the Piper Alpha platform on 6 July 1988?

"What should be recommended with a view to the preservation of life and the avoidance of similar accidents in the future?"

Cullen called 260 witnesses. Fifty-eight of the sixty-one survivors testified. Three men were still enduring skin grafts for their burns and dictated statements for the record. The recollections of most of the survivors in the witness chair were interrupted by raw emotional moments during which Cullen declared recesses until the men regained their footing. Cullen also subpoenaed Grampian policemen; the captains and crew of *Tharos, Silver Pit, Lowland Cavalier, Sandhaven, Maersk Cutter,* and *Loch Shuna,* the television camera crew; helicopter pilots; an insurance executive from Lloyds of London; Occidental International chairman J. E. Brading; the OIMs of Tartan, Claymore, and MCP-01; and experts on explosions, gas leaks, valves, pumps, pipelines, burns, toxic chemicals, electricity, and communications. From photographs and the Grampian TV videotape, it was obvious that the first fire erupted on the production deck. Cullen ordered models built of that part of the rig. When testimony of the witnesses pointed to the possibility of a gas leak in the plumbing of the condensate injection pumps and valves, he ordered full-size replicas built and tested. Cullen went to Flotta to look at the accommodation module. He flew to Claymore and *Tharos* and circled the remains of Piper Alpha, the jagged scar rising from the sea, guarded by boats still patrolling for bodies.

Midway through the inquiry, the energy secretary gave Occidental permission to topple the remains of Piper Alpha into the North Sea. Cullen did not object. The standing wreckage and debris on the seafloor would not shed enough new light on the disaster to justify the risk of trying to explore them any longer. The families of missing men objected vehemently. Their loved ones might still be entombed in wreckage that was going to be treated like industrial junk. Fishermen protested that Occidental's plan would leave a 225-foot tall stump of the steel jacket on the bottom that would foul nets and lines for generations to come. When the oilmen came to Scotland, they had promised that when the oil was gone they would leave the sea as it was before they arrived. People frightened about the release of polychlorinated biphenyls—PCBs—and radioactivity from instruments and other equipment held protest demonstrations. Oxy prevailed. The environmentalists had grown weary after twenty years of losing to the oil companies on the North Sea. On March 28, 1989, tugboats pulled in opposite directions on cables bolted to the remains of Piper Alpha. Underwater explosive charges wired to the legs detonated, sending rainbowed spray into the bright spring morning. Ten seconds later, Piper Alpha was gone.

The answer to Lord Cullen's first question—What caused the disaster?—took the better part of a year to shape itself from the testimony of witnesses and the re-creation of the conditions aboard Piper Alpha on the night it blew. The testimony of Erland Grieve, the only survivor at the scene of the first explosion, was critical. At the shift change four hours before the blast, Occidental production bosses Harold Flook and Bob Vernon did not confirm that the work on pressure safety valve (PSV) 504 was finished. It was in one of the pipes feeding gas to power the two critical condensate injection pumps. If the work on the valve had been completed, it would have been replaced and functional. Because the work was not finished, the valve had not been put back on the pipe. Flook and Vernon were not aware that the opening where the valve should have been was covered by a metal plate, bolted on but not gas-tight.

The alarm sounded in the control room telling Vernon and Geoff Bollands that condensate injection pump B, the only one running at the time, had shut down. Ordinarily, they would have just started the other condensate injection pump A, but they knew it was powered by gas that would flow through pressure safety valve 504 if they turned it on. Vernon had paused. He was not sure if that valve was ready for service. Vernon went down to the production deck in C Module, where he, Bob Richard, and Erland Grieve tried and failed to restart pump B. Without at least one of the injection pumps running, Vernon was going to have to shut down Piper Alpha. It was a decision he loathed making more than any other. Vernon ran back to the control room to look for the paperwork on pump A. He found none and assumed that the work on PSV 504 had been completed. Back on the production deck, Vernon, Richard, and Grieve tried to start pump B one more time. Nothing. When they attempted to start pump A, the gas flowed from the temporarily covered hole in the pipeline where the PSV 504 valve would have been and into the air surrounding the condensate pumps. The gas hovered in a deadly invisible fog covering the production deck until a spark ignited it when the men tried to restart the pump.

The first explosion came moments later, the horrific thud that collapsed the screen in the cinema, the walls in staterooms a hundred feet above, and the ceiling of the dive office forty feet below. Thousands of gallons of diesel fuel in tanks nearby ignited, producing the thick black smoke that characterized the fire after the initial blast. The second, third, and fourth explosions were no mystery. The big pipelines from Tartan, MCP-01, and Claymore successively melted down in increasingly intense heat and ignited their pressurized gas with catastrophic results. Had the rigs feeding those pipelines shut down and depressurized when the first explosion happened on the production deck, the pipelines probably would not have blown and far fewer men would have been killed.

Occidental's safeguard against such a deadly administrative error was called the permit to work system. It was a hedge against incompatibly dangerous work going on at the same time in the same place. Welding near painting. Hoisting steel over men working on deck. Changing a valve on an active gas pipeline. Before starting a job, a worker had to go to the control room and get a permit to work that was then checked against other permits to work to be sure there was no conflict. The supervisors' briefings when they reported for duty included updates on all permits, so one shift knew what the other was doing. Every offshore oil rig had a similar system, designed and imposed by its home office. On some rigs, the system was a religion. On Piper Alpha, it had become perfunctory. The men relied as much on anecdotal knowledge of what was happening as they did on the paperwork. Among the institutional failures Cullen pointed out in his report was Occidental's lackadaisical training and enforcement of the permit to work system.

The investigation revealed other flaws and failures that helped kill 167 men. The firefighting deluge system was switched to manual at the time of the first explosion because divers were working near the water intake pipes. Even if the system had triggered automatically, it probably wouldn't have done much to put out the fire. For months, Occidental and most of the men on the rig had known that the firefighting nozzles and plumbing were clogged with rust and lime scaling. If the system had triggered automatically and hadn't been clogged, it might have doused the flames of the initial diesel oil fire before the gas pipelines ignited and doomed the rig.

Cullen devoted a chapter of his report to the use of an aging fishing trawler, *Silver Pit,* as a safety standby vessel, stating that it was a token gesture by Occidental to conform only to the letter of the law. Its searchlight was not working. The bow thruster and main engine were so decrepit that both broke down during the rescue attempt. Cullen cited the heroism of the crew of *Silver Pit*'s Z-boat, but the old trawler was hopelessly unsuited for its job. "I am entirely satisfied that *Silver Pit* was essentially unsuitable for the purpose of effecting the rescue of survivors. This led in a number of instances to distress and delay in the process of recovering of survivors."

Cullen's report was rife with other condemnations of Occidental and its managers.

"Occidental was too easily satisfied that the permit to work system was being operated correctly, relying on the absence of any feedback that there were problems as indicating that all was well."

"The platform managers did not show the necessary determination to ensure that its men were well trained in safety procedures."

"Occidental management should have been more aware of the need for a high standard of incident prevention and firefighting."

"Inspections by the Department of Energy were superficial and did not reveal clear-cut and readily ascertainable deficiencies."

Cullen's most sweeping condemnation was that Occidental, the other offshore oil companies, their contractors, and government overseers were guilty of promoting a culture of secrecy and blame offshore. The mistrust between the men working for contractors and the men working for the company that owned an oil rig destroyed the cooperation that was essential for responding to an emergency. The existence of Black Lists, White Lists, and the chance that a man's career offshore might be ended without appeal forced silence when men knew their rigs were dangerous. Men offshore were at grave risk every time they went to work because the oil companies and the British government had the same goal: produce as much oil and gas as quickly as possible. Cullen urged the reorganization of government oversight of the offshore oil industry, transferring control from the Department of Energy to the Human Services Executive, which guarded the rights and safety of other industrial workers.

Occidental had already paid survivors and families of the dead a total of $200 million in settlements, most from its own cash reserves. They settled the claims with two stipulations: Occidental admitted no guilt or negligence, and Occidental reserved the right to sue each of the contractors whose men worked on Piper Alpha to recover their money on the grounds that the contractors, not Occidental, were responsible for their employees. Occidental's insurance paid out another $20 million to the survivors and families who were company employees, most of it from corporate insurance. Lloyds of London was on the hook for $3.5 billion for the construction of a rig to replace Piper Alpha. At least 300 million barrels of crude still lay in the subterranean reservoirs of Armand Hammer's Elephant.

A month after Cullen published his conclusions, Scottish chief prosecutor Peter Fraser, Lord of Carmyllie, announced that he would bring no criminal charges against Occidental, its contractors, or the government of Great Britain for the Piper Alpha disaster. "Prosecution would require proof of criminal negligence beyond a reasonable doubt," Fraser wrote in his brief denial of demands by survivors and families that Armand Hammer and his employees face charges. "There is insufficient evidence. Many of the key witnesses were killed in the disaster. The findings of Lord Cullen's inquiry were based on inference. His opinion would be only that of any other single witness, and not enough to convict anyone."

Fraser's decision sent a wave of outrage rolling over the ruined lives of the survivors and the families of the dead. "I'm absolutely devastated by this decision," Bob Ballantyne said. "Occidental cannot kill 167 men and just walk away wiping their hands of it. Can it be possible that an oil company and its board of directors can make decisions that result in the deaths of men and there is no law under which they can be prosecuted? There is something drastically wrong with the world that no one who caused this tragedy will see the inside of a jail cell. It's crazy."

The Piper Alpha Families and Survivors Association voted unanimously to continue their fight for criminal prosecution. "If the people who own and manage Occidental are shielded by the law," Ballantyne said, "we have no choice but to try to change the law. If we do not do everything within our power to bring this company to task, it would be a disservice to all the lads who died. People all over the world have to understand that men's lives are the true cost of oil."

"I wish them well," Lord Fraser said when he heard that the association was going to pursue charges of corporate manslaughter. "I stick to my personal view that there are plenty of people who do not want the matter to go further. It is the right of the bereaved people to take it as far as they can, but it is my belief that in legal terms they probably will not get much further."

He was right.

On December 10, 1990, a month after reading Cullen's report and issuing a denial that Occidental Petroleum could have done anything differently to save the lives of the men on Piper Alpha, Armand Hammer died of bone cancer in Los Angeles. He was ninety-two years old. He spent much of the last year of his life defending himself against lawsuits by the children of his third wife, Frances, who had died a year earlier. They claimed that Hammer had tricked their mother out of $400 million to buy part of his art collection. They wanted the money back. In Hammer's obituary, the *New York Times* made no mention of Piper Alpha.

On July 6, 1991, a thousand people gathered in Hazelhead Park west of Aberdeen on a scorching hot summer afternoon to dedicate Sue Jane Taylor's memorial. The lawns, azaleas, roses, and trees of

Hazelhead Park are a spectacular counterpoint to the hard-edged rock that dominates the old city. In the center of a four-acre rose garden in full bloom, the Queen Mother of England tugged a lanyard. A drape fell away. Atop a granite pedestal inscribed in gold leaf with the names of the dead, three heroic bronze offshore oilmen welcome the living who come there for solace. Since the unveiling, not a day has passed when there were not bouquets of flowers, notes, photographs, cans of beer, packs of smokes, or other tender remembrances placed at the base of the monument.

In 1992, Occidental Petroleum sold its North Sea holdings to Elf Aquitaine, a French conglomerate, for $1.35 billion in cash. As part of the deal, Elf assumed debt of $130 million, much of it from judgments Occidental was still contesting with Piper Alpha survivors, families, and contractors. An anonymous source in the Aberdeen office told a reporter that Occidental just didn't want to deal with the costs and time demanded by the endless new safety regulations that followed the disaster. Shortly after announcing its acquisition, Elf said it would complete the construction of Piper Bravo, which had been started by Occidental, to extract the remaining oil from the reservoir below. The new rig came online in the autumn of 1993 a hundred and thirty yards from the patch of ocean where Piper Alpha had stood. The site of the wreckage below is marked by a single yellow buoy.

After recovering from his burns, Erland Grieve went back offshore. He worked for Oxy until they left the North Sea, stayed with Elf Aquitaine until it left, and signed on with Talisman Oil, a Canadian company that eventually bought out Elf. In 2010, Grieve was the OIM on Piper Bravo.

Bob Ballantyne died of cancer on June 15, 2004, survived by his wife, Pat Slater, their two young daughters, and his daughter from a previous marriage with whom he was very close. For fifteen years after the disaster, Ballantyne was the loudest voice of the Piper Alpha Families and Survivors Association, campaigning tirelessly for offshore workingmen who worked in conditions he compared with those of nineteenth-century Welsh coal mines. Ballantyne never ceased to believe that the Piper Alpha disaster was the result of the priorities of the free-market capitalism promoted by the

Thatcher government during the oil-boom years at the expense of working people.

Bill Barron lives quietly in Aberdeen with Trish and two cocker spaniels in a house not far from the cottage on the River Don where he dug his holes. He runs a small landscaping business, hunts pigeons and pheasants in the fall, and spends most afternoons shooting pool in the bar of the Buckie Farm restaurant across the street from his house. After posing for Sue Jane Taylor, Barron loaned labor leader Ronnie MacDonald £10,000 when he was trying to organize the Offshore Oil Liaison Committee. Less than 5 percent of offshore workers are now members of trade unions.

Dick Common, Barry Barber's clerk in the dive complex on Piper Alpha, killed himself in 1994. He was a single man who felt terrible guilt for surviving when Barber, who had a wife and children, died. "I know without a doubt that he died because of Piper Alpha," a friend of his told a reporter after Common's body was found in his apartment. "It never left his mind. It was a nightmare that went on and on."

In 1998, a month after the tenth anniversary of the disaster, Dr. David Alexander, who had counseled the policemen recovering bodies from the accommodation module, began a study into the long-term psychological effects of Piper Alpha. Thirty-six survivors gave interviews or completed questionnaires. Almost all of them reported psychological problems. Twenty-eight said they were willing to work offshore again but had trouble finding jobs after the disaster. The oil companies and contractors regarded Piper Alpha survivors as Jonahs, bringers of bad luck who were not welcome on the rigs. More than 70 percent of the men said they had feelings of acute guilt. Many felt they should not have survived when equally or more deserving men perished. Some of them went on to play what Alexander described as "Russian roulette" with their lives. They drove fast and recklessly and took dangerous jobs. "Unconsciously, they were looking for ways to be punished for the fact that they came through relatively unharmed while other men died. Some of them said they were stronger than they were before Piper Alpha. They learned things about themselves, changed their values, some relationships became stronger," Alexander said. "They realized they have strengths they didn't know they had. A lot of heroism took place out there that night."

Ed Punchard now lives on the Indian Ocean in Western Australia, as far from the North Sea as he can be without leaving the planet. He and Vicky divorced a year after Piper Alpha, but he stayed with his therapy for post-traumatic stress disorder. Punchard finished his book, *Piper Alpha: A Survivor's Story,* with the help of writer Syd Higgins. He then made a television documentary, *Paying for the Piper,* that led him into a career as a filmmaker. Punchard remains fiercely committed to revealing the abominable safety record of the offshore oil industry. He never turns down an invitation to tell his story. At the twentieth anniversary commemoration of the disaster in 2008, he returned to Aberdeen, where he announced the creation of a fund for 167 scholarships for children of offshore oil workers in honor of Piper Alpha's dead.

Elf, the company that bought Occidental's North Sea field, sold *Tharos* to Transocean, a drilling company that converted it for extreme deepwater work and renamed it the *Transocean Marianas.* In November 2009, Hurricane Ida slammed into the Gulf of Mexico, damaging it so badly that it had to be replaced by the *Deepwater Horizon.* Four months later, the *Deepwater Horizon* was drilling in water five thousand feet deep when a blowout preventer failed, killing eleven men, sinking the rig, and triggering the worst oil spill in history.

Acknowledgments

What matters most in my acknowledgment of the many contributions to this book is the remembrance here of the 162 men of Piper Alpha who died, as well as the survivors, the families and friends of all of them, and the brave men and women who tended to this agony as rescuers, comforters, and witnesses. This is their story, and it is my privilege to tell it.

Writing about a catastrophe twenty years after the fact required that I ask many of the living to summon to mind the worst thing that ever happened to them. It was a request that is an abomination on its face, but one to which all responded with grace and kindness. I was admitted into the lives of people whose recollections about Piper Alpha and the night of July 6, 1988, form the heart of this book. My expression of gratitude to them here is a meager recognition of their immense help. Thank you Ken Clarke, Dennis Davidson, John Fuller, Ann Gillanders, Elspeth Murray Graham, Bill Mackie, Peter Mitchell, Jake Moloy, Mike McCaig, Archie Robb, and Toby Swift. Bill Barron opened his life to me with unrestrained vulnerability and enriched my perception of the practical details of getting off a burning oil rig. Sue Jane Taylor's paintings, photographs, and recollections inspired me and informed my perspectives on life offshore to such a degree that I could not have told this story without her. Ed Punchard's book, *Piper Alpha: A Survivor's Story*, is a testament to the fierce spirit of a man who could have abandoned his life to misery but instead prevailed heroically. His further willingness to talk openly with me about his life before, during, and after Piper Alpha was a true gift.

The usual suspects in Port Townsend provided me with friendship and great food. Thank you Karen Childers, Rich Childers, Bill Curtsinger, John Dorgan, Rikki Ducornet, Greg Friedrichs, Caroline Gibson, Amy Grondin, Max Grover, Charlie Hansen, Lucy Congden Hansen, Guy Hupy, Joel Kawahara, Mark Miller, Tulip Morrow, Sue Ohlson, Roger Steinfort, and Walt Trisdale. Many other friends gave me advice and comfort. Thank you Sally Anderson, Mark Brinster, Arthur Coburn, Will Nothdurft, Carol Ostrom, Kate Pflaumer, Eric Scigliano, Mark Shelley, Glen Sims, and Ray Troll. Paul Shukovsky's wisdom as a grief counselor was essential to my respectful encounters with the survivors and loved ones of Piper Alpha's dead.

Richard Abate, maestro and agent, found the story of Piper Alpha and led me through its creation with patience and his incredible sense of drama in the telling. He has been a force of nature in my life for a decade, and I wake up grateful to him every day. I am also grateful to Richard's associates Shawn Coyne and Melissa Kahn for their kindnesses.

Thank you again, Edward Kastenmeier, for your editorial skill and for bringing me to Pantheon Books ten years ago. Working with you has been among the great rewards of my writing life. Thanks also to Tim O'Connell, Emily Giglierano, and the wizards in the back room at Pantheon who contributed so much without fanfare to the production of this book.

My daughter, Laara, and my grandson, Milo, enrich my life with their love. Barbara Manchester, my beloved comrade and first reader, inspired my work and reassured me that beauty exists in every moment of life. This book would not have found its truth without her.

Brad Matsen
Port Townsend, Washington

Bibliography

Alvarez, A. *Offshore: A North Sea Journey.* London: Hodder and Stoughton, 1986.

Blumay, Carl, with Henry Edwards. *The Dark Side of Power: The Real Armand Hammer.* New York: Simon and Schuster, 1992.

Cullen, Hon. Lord William Douglas. *The Public Inquiry into the Piper Alpha Disaster.* London: British Department of Energy, 1990.

Dunning, Fred, and Ian F. Mercer et al. *Britain's Offshore Oil and Gas,* 2nd ed. London: U.K. Offshore Operators Association, 2002.

Fyvie, John F. *Flight of the Paraffin Budgie: A North Sea Chronicle.* Aberdeen (self-published), 1989.

Hammer, Armand, with Neil Lyndon. *Hammer.* New York: G. P. Putnam's Sons, 1987.

Hewison, W. S. *The Great Harbour: Scapa Flow.* Edinburgh: Birlinn, 2005.

Lovell, Jim, and Jeffrey Kluger. *Lost Moon: The Perilous Voyage of* Apollo 13. New York: Houghton Mifflin, 1994.

Mackie, Bill. *The Klondykers: The Oilmen Onshore.* Edinburgh: Birlinn, 2006.

———*The Oilmen: The North Sea Tigers.* Edinburgh: Birlinn, 2004.

Margonelli, Lisa. *Oil on the Brain: Petroleum's Long, Strange Trip to Your Tank.* New York: Doubleday, 2007.

Matthiessen, Peter. *Men's Lives: The Surfmen and Baymen of the South Fork.* New York: Random House, 1986.

McGinty, Stephen. *Fire in the Night: The Piper Alpha Disaster.* London: Macmillan, 2008.

Mostert, Noel. *Supership.* New York: Alfred A. Knopf, 1974.

Punchard, Ed, with Syd Higgins. *Piper Alpha: A Survivor's Story.* London: W. H. Allen, 1989.

Smith, David. *Aberdeen in the Fifties and Sixties.* Derby, Scotland: Breeden Books, 2001.

Talese, Gay. *The Bridge.* New York: Walker and Company, 2003.

Taylor, Sue Jane. *Oilwork: North Sea Diaries.* Edinburgh: Birlinn, 2005.

Weinberg, Steve. *Armand Hammer: The Untold Story.* Boston: Little, Brown, 1989.

Woolfson, Charles, John Foster, and Mathias Beck. *Paying for the Piper: Capital and Labour in Britain's Offshore Oil Industry.* London: Mansell, 1996.

Yergin, Daniel. *The Prize: The Epic Quest for Oil, Money and Power.* New York: Simon and Schuster, 1992.

Index

ABOUT THE AUTHOR

Brad Matsen is the author of *Jacques Cousteau,* Titanic's *Last Secrets, Descent: The Heroic Discovery of the Abyss,* and many other books about the sea and its inhabitants. He was a creative producer for the television series *The Shape of Life,* and his articles on marine science and the environment have appeared in *Mother Jones, Audubon,* and *Natural History,* among other publications. He lives in Port Townsend, Washington.

A NOTE ON THE TYPE

The text of this book was set in Sabon, a typeface designed by Jan Tsch-ichold (1902–1974), the well-known German typographer. Designed in 1966 and based on the original designs by Claude Garamond (ca. 1480–1561), Sabon was named for the punch cutter Jacques Sabon, who brought Garamond's matrices to Frankfurt.

Composed by North Market Street Graphics
Lancaster, Pennsylvania

Printed and bound by Berryville Graphics
Berryville, Virginia

Designed by M. Kristen Bearse